Praise for Nancy I. Sanders and *Yes! You Can*

Here, at last, is the book on children's writing I've been looking for to offer my writing customers. Covers the gamut of information and encouragement a children's writer needs to crack this market—whether a beginner or more experienced. Well-organized and easy to read.

— Sally E. Stuart, Christian Writers' Market Guide, www.stuartmarket.com

I'm 100% behind the idea of an alternate approach to the publication journey as my own publishing road has been anything but normal. This book offers a solid guide to publication for any writer looking for an eventual career in writing and willing to try a road slightly less traveled.

— Jan Fields, Editor of *Kid Magazine Writers* ezine and the Children's Writers eNews, www.kidmagwriters.com

Fresh. Practical. Honest. These are the terms which best describe Nancy's book on writing for children. It's unlike any other book on this topic that I've seen. If you don't succeed as a children's writer after studying this book and doing what it says, you probably need to stick with some other genre. The content in this book is awesome!

— Sandy Brooks, Director, Christian Writers Fellowship International, www.cwfi-online.org/

Some writers write about what they know while other writers write about what they know and do. Nancy does what she writes about. She has tested and proven what she writes about. Although this book is focused on writing for children, it contains valuable nuggets for any writer.

— Reg A. Forder, Founder/Director of American Christian Writers, www.ACWriters.com

D1564244

Nancy I. Sanders is one of those unique individuals who can write creatively in such a manner that causes individuals to want to read what she has to say! She is a practitioner, having proven herself as an author of multiple works. *Yes! You Can* is saturated with practical tips for organizing oneself by setting attainable goals, connecting with other writers, and discovering how to reach out successfully to publishers. The book is extremely readable, yet it oozes with proven actions the writer can take to become a successful author of children's to young adults' books.

— Raymond E. White, Ed.D., Project Coordinator for *The Reading Project*, Downey Child Care Center, Downey, California

If you want to learn how to write, sell and market a blockbuster, you should read this book. If you also want to produce a body of work, build a solid career and make a living as a writer, you *must* read this book. It is a goldmine of information on every aspect of the writing craft. With plenty of insider tips and examples, the author demystifies manuscript preparation, queries, proposals, age range, controlled vocabulary, ghostwriting, work-for-hire, literary contracts and much, much more. In *Yes! You Can*, Nancy I. Sanders provides a road map that will help a writer take control of his or her career, get out of the slush pile, and turn the dream into reality.

— Q. L. Pearce, Author of more than 150 books for children

I highly recommend *Yes! You Can* to writers of all levels. Nancy I. Sanders' commonsense techniques and helpful tips can turn any writer into a success. How do I know? I landed my first picture book contract by applying her methods. If I can, you can, too!

— Catherine L. Osornio, Children's Book Author and Freelance Writer, www.catherinelosornio.wordpress.com

If you enjoy writing for children, but you're not sure what to do next, then this is the book for you! Nancy I. Sanders writes from personal experience, and shares with you the path to a successful and satisfying writing career. This is a realistic, doable, and encouraging handbook for any author who is ready to get published.

— Veronica Walsh, illustrator for *Too Many Visitors for One Little House,* www.veronicawalsh.net

I bet I would have been a full-time writer many years sooner if *Yes! You Can* had been published when I was starting my writing career. It's full of practical advice, clear explanations, step-by-step plans, and plenty of encouragement. I especially love the way specific tips are offered depending on whether the reader is a full-time or low-time writer, as well as tips for both new writers and file-cabinets-full-of-unpublished-manuscripts writers. The Triple Crown of Success approach is fantastic! It helps me clarify, even at this stage, the balancing act I struggle with as a writer who loves to write but who also must make a livable income. *Yes! You Can* is a must-have for any writer trying to build a bona fide writing career! I'll be recommending it to all my writing students.

— Laura Purdie Salas, *Stampede! Poems to Celebrate the Wild Side of School* and more than 80 other books for kids, www.laurasalas.com

Want to discover how to become a successful children's book author? Valuable insider tips are here. Nancy I. Sanders' smart and engaging guidelines take all the guesswork out of achieving your goals. *Yes! You Can* provides the ultimate strategy to getting you published and keeping you on the right track to a satisfying writing career.

— Francesca Rusackas is the author of the award-winning picture book, *I Love You All Day Long.*

Finally! A practical guide to realizing the goals of a children's writer—get published, earn an income, and write for fulfillment. Nancy I. Sanders provides the tools to start and manage a rewarding career. Tips on subjects such as getting the most from a critique group, achieving short and long-term objectives, and targeting publishers, are included with essential information on writing for every age-level in the children's market. This book is a blueprint for how to succeed as an author while having fun along the way.

— Rilla Jaggia, Children's Author, Editor—*Kite Tales*— Newsletter for the SCBWI Tri-Regions of Southern California, www.rillajaggia.com

Follow the advice given in Nancy I. Sanders' book and your chances of becoming a published author more than quadruple! I was one of those writers who only wrote when I got an inspiration. Then I searched for publishers who might like what I wrote. Nancy has taught me to get the contract BEFORE I write the book. On my first try at doing this, I was contacted by a publisher and asked to send a partial manuscript. Needless to say, I became a believer! Read her book, follow the advice, and see how wide the doors of the publishing world open for you, too.

— Gloria McQueen Stockstill, Speaker and Author of four board books including *The Basket in the River, To the Town of Bethlehem, The Blind Man by the Road,* and *Jesus Rose on Easter Morn,* www.gloriastockstill.blogspot.com

If anyone has earned the right to help others become writers, it's Nancy I. Sanders. A prolific author herself, Nancy has a gift of communicating to her readers in simple, practical, and engaging ways, motivating even the most insecure among us to say, "I can do this!"

— Kim Kautzer, Author/Publisher, *WriteShop,* www.writeshop.com

Without a doubt, Nancy I. Sanders is one of the finest examples of our time on how to teach the special skills needed to become a published children's writer! She leads by true example and offers something that is often difficult for writers to see—HOPE! This book is an outstanding resource. Please don't miss it! Nancy, your precious friendship and mentoring through the years have changed me forever!

— Sheryl Crawford has coauthored seven Scholastic Professional Books with Nancy I. Sanders. Her published books include *Easy-to-Read Science Plays about the Human Body* (Scholastic), *Psalms for a Child's Heart* and *The Baby Who Changed the World* (Faithkidz), and *My Little Prayers* (Word/contributing author). Visit Sheryl's blog (Sherri Tales) at www.sherylcrawford.blogspot.com.

Stop! Don't read this book if you have no desire to be a successful children's writer. If you are determined to continue, then proceed at your own risk—this book is dynamite! It will tunnel you through Slushpile Mountain past all but the outskirts of Rejectionville, and bring you to the happy city of Published Writer. Nancy I. Sanders leads you on a unique yet common-sense journey that will keep you on the write track. I'd say more but I must hurry to enrich my own writing by studying this fabulous book again.

— Shirley Shibley, Children's Author with stories in several periodicals including *Clubhouse* and *Bread for God's Children* magazines, and over 75 stories and articles accepted for book compilations being published for private schools

Nancy I. Sanders is a skilled and successful freelance writer who knows what she wants and goes after it. She's uncovered the secret to what really works in getting published, often flying in the face of traditional advice! In *Yes! You Can* she shares, in a very practical way, the many strategies that have brought her to the level of earning she enjoys today. The sub-headings in each chapter help the reader zero in on specific information, and the "Beginners' Tip" and "Professional Track" notations make this book ideal for anyone who wants to win at the writing game.

— Marjorie Flathers, Freelance Writer and Contributor to the Kids' Reading Room page of the *Los Angeles Times*.

If you have always wanted to write for children, *Yes! You Can* by Nancy I. Sanders is the book that will lead you, step by step, along the road to success. Learn how to turn your weaknesses into strengths! Earn while you learn! Create a writing schedule that works for you! From story ideas to signed contracts, all the information you need is within these pages. You might have to put this book down so that you can begin your own writing, but I guarantee that you will pick it up again . . . and again.

— Marilyn Cram-Donahue is the author of 31 books and over 500 articles and short stories. She facilitates critique groups, serves as a career advisor for Pomona College, and is a consultant to the National Writing Project. Currently, she is working on two novels and a memoir. Visit her at marilyndonahue@wordpress.com.

Nancy I. Sanders' inspiring coaching already has me in the sweatpants of daily writing running up the publishing stairs of success. Her new book, *Yes! You Can* from E & E Publishing is just what I need to get my writing to start paying for my dreams, instead of my dreams paying the high price of being a writer. Her "easy peasy" suggestions will have you shouting "yippee skippy" when you're up to your ears in crocodiles (or bills). Nancy knows that to be a successful children's writer, you're going to need to have fun! Her idea for a personal writing notebook to record ideas for characters like Mindalyn McGookin and putting on your editor's hat have the child in the children's writer dancing around the room to the tune of "you can."

— Sharon Riddle, Author and Owner of Olive Leaf Publications, www.oliveleafpublications.com

Yes! You Can

Learn How To
Write
Children's Books,

Get Them
Published,

and Build a
$uccessful
Writing Career

Nancy I. Sanders

E & E Publishing
Sausalito, California

E & E Publishing,
a Registered Trade Name of
THE E & E GROUP LLC
1001 Bridgeway, No. 227
Sausalito, California 94965
U.S.A.
Website: www.EandEGroup.com/Publishing
Email: EandEGroup@EandEGroup.com

Publisher's Cataloging-In-Publication Data
(Prepared by The Donohue Group, Inc.)

Sanders, Nancy I.
    Yes! you can : learn how to write children's books, get them published, and build a successful writing career / Nancy I. Sanders.

        p. ; cm.

    Includes index.
    ISBN-13: 978-0-9791606-6-0
    ISBN-10: 0-9791606-6-9

    1. Children's literature--Technique--Handbooks, manuals, etc.
    2. Children's literature--Authorship--Handbooks, manuals, etc.
    3. Children's literature--Publishing--Handbooks, manuals, etc.
    I. Title.

PN147.5 .S26 2009
808/.06/8

Printed in U.S.A.

If one can, anyone can.

If two can, you can, too!™

Dedication

I want to dedicate this book to my awesome online picture book critique group, "Pens and Brushes." What a great community you are for professional advice, uplifting encouragement, and all-around fun. You guys are the best! A big, extra-special thank-you and lots of hugs go to Mirka M. G. Breen, Mark Ceilley, Tina M. Cho, Evelyn Christensen, Joshua W. Hawkins, Diane Hower (and Stanley, the Read-Aloud dog!), and Priya Iyengar. May all our writing dreams come true!

Acknowledgements

A special appreciation goes to Tina M. Cho who diligently and enthusiastically provided superior feedback on each chapter of the book. Tina, your perspective encouraged me and helped me polish each page. Thanks for your hard work. Also, heartfelt thanks go to Laurie Fuller and Renee Gray-Wilburn, who willingly stepped up to the plate to provide helpful feedback, as well.

I am especially grateful for publisher Eve Heidi Bine-Stock at E & E Publishing. Eve, your how-to books for picture book writers meet a vital need for children's writers as well as greatly influenced the development of my own picture book writing skills.

When you caught the vision for this new book, it took my breath away. It's been a joy working together with you each step of this incredible journey.

Table of Contents

Introduction

Just because you're not a gourmet chef in your own restaurant, doesn't mean you can't cook. There are countless numbers of successful cooks working in a wide variety of venues. Think of Mrs. Fields® Cookies, Cinnabon, your favorite hot dog stand, and perhaps even your very own aunt's catering business.

Just because you're not a bestselling children's book author, doesn't mean you can't write. There are countless numbers of successful children's writers working in a variety of markets. Think of *National Geographic Kids* magazine, school textbooks, craft books, puzzle books, and even cookbooks for kids.

Yes! You can experience success as a children's writer even if you don't yet know how to craft a great story. While you're learning the storytelling tricks of the trade, you can start getting published right away. While you're polishing your skills at creating unforgettable characters and believable dialogue, you can start earning income as a children's writer. I'll show you how as you read through the pages of this book.

Reality Check #1

This industry is full of huge publishers that are hard to break into. The good news? There are lots of smaller publishers practically begging for manuscripts from first-time authors. I'll teach you where to look and how to connect with them.

Reality Check #2

It can take years to get published. The good news? Just like someone needs to work at your favorite hot dog stand around the corner, there are plenty of opportunities to get published in today's market. You can start getting published right away. I'll show you how.

Reality Check #3

This industry is filled with frustrated writers who can't earn a living writing for children. The good news? There are actually lots of people who maintain a successful part-time or full-time career as a children's writer. I do and I know others who do, too. In these chapters, I'll share strategies on how you can join the ranks.

Yes! You can get published, learn how to be successful, and earn a decent income as a children's writer. Not overnight...not for quick cash...and not in a haphazard way. Whether it's to create your own line of cookies or to help with your aunt's catering business, you can make it happen. And with a careful strategy, determined mindset, and strong self-motivation, you can build the successful children's writing career of your dreams. In this book, I'll show you how to start.

The advice you'll find here comes from practical experience in the real world of children's publishing. I'm sharing the strategies and techniques that work for me. If you implement these into your own journey, I'm confident that you can have a solid foundation for building a successful career as a children's writer.

Today, when I speak to other writers about the strategies I use, someone always says, "This works for you because you're an established writer."

But these methods worked for me when I wasn't.

Someone inevitably suggests, "You sign so many contracts today because you've written so many books already."

But I followed many of these same techniques when I published my very first book...and my second.

Someone else might say, "You experience success because you're a talented writer."

But I experienced success as a beginning writer when I didn't even know what I was doing. The majority of manuscripts I worked on underwent heavy revisions during the editorial process. Since revision is a natural part of every manuscript's journey, the editors were used to it.

The tips and advice you read about in this book will probably be different from everything you've heard about writing for children. How do I know? I've got most of the leading "how to write for children" books on my bookshelves. The majority of these books spend the greatest portion of the book explaining how to be a master storyteller and polish your manuscript until it shines. Then these books tell you to begin your search for the perfect publisher. I've attended writer's conferences and networked with editors and sat in writing classes. The majority focus on how to write fiction for children and revise your manuscript to perfection. Then they send you off to research for the right publisher or agent. That works for some, but it wasn't the right path for me.

Here, in my book, I will show you a different way.

I will teach you how to find a publisher first before you ever write one single word of your manuscript. I will teach you how to earn income while you're learning how to write a story because you're writing an article or book as an assignment or under a signed contract. I will teach you the strategies many career writers use to earn money that increases their income and pays their bills. I will teach you how to build a successful career as a children's writer.

Just a word of caution, however. You may read something in this book and gulp, "That's _not_ what my writing instructor told me!"

Has your writing instructor helped you land a book contract yet? Or two or three?

Perhaps you'll read a technique here within these pages and gasp, "That's _not_ what the top editor at the writer's conference said!"

Did that editor accept your book manuscript and publish it even after you followed her step-by-step instructions to submit your manuscript to her?

Maybe you'll read my advice in this book and argue, "That's <u>not</u> what the writers in my critique group tell me!"

Are any of them earning between $20,000 and $70,000 a year as a children's writer?

If you answered "No" to any of these questions, what have you got to lose? Go ahead! Try my advice and see what happens. I did this, and it worked for me. You can try it, too. Yes, you can!

Beginner's Tip

You'll be surprised at how far you can go and how much you can accomplish if you just believe that you can.

Professional Track

Try an experiment. Imagine you're a brand new writer and haven't yet learned a thing about the world of writing for kids. With this fresh, open attitude, turn the page and continue reading. Implement the strategies I suggest. Try each one on for size. Keep on going until you reach the end of this book. Then take off, and soar into the writing career of your dreams.

Chapter 1
The Career of Writing for Children

1.1 Do You Really Want to be a Children's Writer?

Chances are, if you dream about being a children's writer, you probably loved to read as a child, are drawn to the intrigue and thrill of a story, or are a natural storyteller. You might want to write stories for your own children to read or to leave an important legacy. Perhaps you've always dreamed about being an author. You even might feel a longing to satisfy your inner child. Writing for children awakens a sense of innocence and wonder that is somehow different than writing for any other audience. What a wonderful imagination you probably have! I'm so excited that you're reading this book. I want to share with you the tips and techniques that have worked for me so that you can take all those creative juices that are bubbling up inside you and become the writer you long to be.

If you really want to be a children's writer, let me encourage you. I started out knowing *nothing* about the business of writing. I didn't know about writers' conferences, critique groups, market guides, publishing houses, agents, queries or book proposals. I didn't know how to type a manuscript in its proper format. I didn't even know the word "submissions" meant to send something to an editor—I just typed up my story and mailed it to the first magazine that came to mind!

Yet, little-by-little, step-by-step, I moved forward in pursuit of my dreams of one day being a published author. And now I am. With over 75 books published in houses big and small, I am a career writer landing three or more new book contracts every year for the last ten to fifteen years.

Often, when I speak at a local writer's event, someone says, "Well, you can land a book contract because you're already established." I try to remind them that I started at square one, just like most of us do.

If you're interested in becoming a writer, one of the best things you can do is find an activity that gets you writing fresh material every day. I don't mean "writing" as in working on a magazine article or book manuscript. Write every day in a journal. Keep a diary. Start a blog. Write your family's memoirs. Write detailed letters to long-distance family and friends. By sitting down to write every day like this, it builds up your stamina for writing. It trains your brain to craft sentences and form complete thoughts. It develops your ability to communicate your ideas through the written word.

I know far too many people who dream about writing. They talk about writing. They read about writing. They edit and rehash and rework manuscripts that they've been carrying around for ten years. They belong to two or more critique groups. They read other people's blogs and purchase the newest writer's markets every year. There's nothing wrong with any of those activities. But I don't see evidence of their actually sitting down to write new material.

If you sit down each day, however, for at least fifteen minutes and "allow" your brain to enjoy the process of uninhibited writing in your journal, diary, blog, memoirs, or personal letters, your writer's soul will be fed. It will grow. It will mature. You will come to realize you *are* a writer and that you're on your way to learning to express your thoughts to the world through the written word.

So, be encouraged. Take heart! Put on your writer's hat and sit down to write. Today. Step-by-step, day-by-day, you can work toward making your dreams come true. Read the next section to find out more.

Beginner's Tip

To get the most out of this book, it might help to read it quickly through from cover-to-cover first. Then come back and read slowly through each section, digesting the concepts and putting the suggestions into action.

Professional Track

Chances are, by now you've read plenty of how-to books about writing. Much of the advice in this book might be very different from what you've heard elsewhere. That's because these steps are the steps that work for me. If they seem strange, don't be afraid to try them. Perhaps they'll work for you, too.

1.2 Learn to Explore

Do you love the art of storytelling? Do you treasure childhood memories of reading a beautiful picture book? Do you desire to join the ranks of influential children's authors who have led each new generation of youth down through the hallowed halls of history? I do, and I'm sure you do, too. The great news is that there isn't some mystical, magical formula that will help you live the writer's life of your dreams. You can take practical steps to learn how to write and learn to write well. You, too, can be a children's writer.

One thing you may have noticed by now if you've already started to get plugged into the world of writing for children is that the main theme of most writers' conferences, critique groups, and writing books is how to become a master storyteller in the mainstream market.

To be honest, it scared me at first. It still does. You see, even though I delight in the art of storytelling, it doesn't come naturally to me. My husband, on the other hand, is a natural-born storyteller. He keeps us spellbound as he weaves a story just to share what happened at his work. He's naturally gifted at telling a story. Not me.

Even though I have wonderful childhood memories of reading all the great classics, I didn't have a clue how to write one when I first decided to write. I'd read *Little Women* perched high up in an apple tree on the dairy farm in Everett, Pennsylvania where I grew up. I laughed myself silly over Winnie-the-Pooh's wonderful, tongue-tickling, rollicking antics. I even read *Pride and Prejudice* aloud with my future sister-in-law while floating on a raft in the middle of our pond one summer when I was a teen. Sure, I knew a good book when I read one. Writing one, myself, was a different story.

If you're shaking in your boots like I was when I started writing, I've got exciting news for you. There are oodles of opportunities for children's writers where you can get published and earn a decent income long before you've learned all the ropes of being a master storyteller. Trust me. I know!

The key word is: *Explore!* After all, exploration is a common ingredient of a child's world. Learn to explore the world of children's publishing. There are many exciting opportunities to write for kids other than a picture book. There are craft books, textbooks, and kid's magazines. There are puzzle books, reader's theater books, and dramatic plays. There are stories for kids in standardized tests, beginning readers, and reproducible books for teachers to use.

Learn to explore your own talents, abilities, and shortcomings as a writer. Children's publishers need countless authors even in today's crowded market to write manuscripts for publications other than a middle grade or young adult novel. Learn to explore who you are and how you can fit into the current publishing market today—even while you're studying and improving your storytelling craft.

It can take years to become a master story-teller. It can take years to learn how to write the perfect setting, develop characters that connect with the hearts of your readers, and create a plot that compels your readers to turn the page. While you're busy learning the art and technique of creating the next bestseller, however, there are numerous avenues to explore in the world of children's publishing that will earn you published credits and an income that pays the bills. In other words, you can build a successful career as a children's writer even if you are not yet a master storyteller. Isn't that encouraging news? Read the following section to find out how to start.

Beginner's Tip

Visit your local bookstore with a pen and notepad. Explore the children's section. Make a list of the different kinds of books you find. Picture books and novels are on the shelves, of course. However, there are also puzzle books, craft books, cookbooks, activity books, educational books, and more. Each different publisher needs a different children's writer to write each different book. Perhaps the next writer could be you!

Professional Track

If you've always wanted to get a picture book or a children's novel published, but have only had success in other areas, make time today to reach for your goal. Put together a special notebook of tips and techniques specifically geared for your favorite genre to help you write the book of your dreams.

1.3 Your Biggest Weakness, Your Greatest Strength

Did you know that C. S. Lewis, author of *The Chronicles of Narnia*, and J. R. R. Tolkien, author of *The Lord of the Rings*, were in the same critique group called the "Inklings"? Both were master storytellers. Can you imagine being a member of their group? As writers it's easy to compare ourselves with other children's writers and wish we had the same strengths as the great literary masters of all time. However, did you know that your greatest weakness as a writer can actually become your greatest strength? You can become the writer you long to be with a successful writing career, and it can start by identifying your greatest weakness.

For instance, do you want to write a middle grade novel, but feel bad because you waste all day reading other writers' blogs instead of actually writing? Turn your greatest weakness into your greatest strength. Contact a writer's e-zine, or online writer's magazine, and ask if they need someone to write a column that spotlights different great writers' blogs each issue. Then, while you're earning money or building published credits writing your column, sign up to take a class on fiction techniques.

Do you long to write a picture book, but spend all day chatting on the phone with your friends instead of writing? Turn your greatest weakness into your greatest strength. Contact a publisher who needs interviews. From local newspapers to community magazines to big-paying teen magazines to work-for-hire book publishers, numerous editors are hungry for interview-based manuscripts. Then, while you're earning money or building published credits writing exciting, on-the-edge interviews, read a how-to book on picture book writing.

Do you want to finish that young adult (YA) novel you started, but feel depressed because you spend hours each day researching market leads and current publishing trends, but never start to type? Turn your greatest weakness into your greatest strength. Contact a writer's magazine or website and ask if they'd like someone to write marketing updates about what manuscripts different publishers are currently looking for. Then, while you're earning money and building published credits writing marketing news, join an online YA critique group to help you be accountable to write that book.

Do you love writing contests and submit to every contest you find, but never actually write your historical fiction novel? Turn your greatest weakness into your greatest strength. Contact any source that offers contests and offer to help write the rules for their next event. Then, while you're earning money and building published credits writing contest rules, join a historical fiction listserve, a specialized e-mail group, bursting with advice on how to write your book.

To find a listserve, also spelled listserv, search online or in places such as Yahoo! Groups. Visit websites of organizations such as the Society of Children's Writers and Illustrators at www.scbwi.org and post messages saying you're interested in finding a historical fiction listserve to join. Network with other writing communities and friends and find a listserve just right for you.

Do you love those writing exercises—but never actually put them into practice in your own novel? Turn your greatest weakness into your greatest strength. Write a book in the educational market for teachers to use in the classroom chock-full of writing prompts. Then, while you're earning money or building published credits writing for the educational market, sign up for an online class on developing the perfect plot.

Do you want to write your nonfiction picture book for kids, but can't attend a critique group for feedback because you've got preschoolers at home? Turn your greatest weakness into your greatest strength. Offer to write a parenting column in your local newspaper or community magazine. Then, while you're earning money or building published credits writing parenting tips, subscribe to a writer's magazine to learn how to write nonfiction with pizzazz.

Learn to identify your weaknesses as a writer, and turn them into your greatest strengths.

For instance, do you feel like quitting because you aren't self-motivated as a writer? You might be the perfect candidate for work-for-hire projects where an editor tells you exactly what to write and when to deliver it to her desk.

Are you worried you can't succeed because you're the type of writer who never gets an original idea? You might thrive as a series writer. That's where you're handed a story bible that provides detailed guidelines of what the story will be all about so that it fits into the other books in that series.

Have you been depressed because you just can't stand working all alone? You might do a wonderful job working at a publishing house where you go to the office each day and work on projects they hand to you to complete.

Do you get the picture? Not every writer is a master storyteller. I'm not, although after all these years of writing, I'm learning how to be one. Along the way, however, I've learned to identify my weaknesses and turn them into projects that earn income and build my published credits. My weaknesses have become my greatest strengths. You can do the same. You can build a successful writing career. To find out what it takes, read the next section.

Beginner's Tip

As you're just getting started on your journey as a writer, be sure to stop now and then to evaluate your newly discovered strengths and weaknesses along the way. Keep asking yourself, "How can I turn my greatest weakness into profit or published credits?" If you're brave, ask for someone else's input.

Professional Track

If you've been depressed because you're trying to conform to some preconceived concept of the "perfect writer," learn to appreciate who you are. There is no other writer in the whole entire universe who views things from your one-of-a-kind perspective. Your writer's heart is as unique as your fingerprint. Stop comparing yourself to other writers. Instead, make a list of your personal strengths as a writer. Ask yourself, "How can I more effectively develop the strengths I already have?"

1.4 Hobby or Career?

You can build a successful career as a children's writer. You might be brand new and just getting started as a writer. Or, you might have been writing for years yet feel like you're spinning your wheels and going nowhere. Whatever your situation has been in the past, you can write children's books, you can get published, and you can earn income. Isn't it exciting to know this? You can!

How do I know? I once heard a phrase, and I believe that it's true:

If one can, anyone can.
If two can, you can, too!™

You see, I've built a successful career as a children's writer. I've gotten published, and I've earned a steady income for years. If I can do it, anyone can do it.

But it's not just me. I know other children's book authors who are building successful careers, too. If two can do it, then so can you. Isn't that wonderful to hear?

This book is all about building a successful career as a children's writer. It's not about a hobby. Oh, it's perfectly fine if you like to write as a hobby. That doesn't mean you're not a writer. It just means you like to write for fun. It's not essential that you earn an income or get published along the way. Sure, it would be great if you could. Many authors write manuscripts with the hopes and dreams of getting published and landing that dream deal with a huge advance, or payment even before the book is published. Some do. You can, too. It's just not a practical way to build a successful career.

If you're interested in establishing a career, it's essential that you earn money and start earning it as soon as possible. I'm confident the strategies and advice in this book will help you accomplish your goals. One of the first things to consider is the following equation:

Time + Work = Income

This equation holds true for most careers, and it's true for the career of writing as well. If you plan to earn income as a writer, it will take time and it will take work. There simply isn't any way of getting around it.

Think about it. If you decided you needed to get a job to pay your bills, you'd probably get hired somewhere, clock into work, and then work for your assigned hours. It takes the same attitude regarding the job of writing. If you want to earn money as a writer, you have to show up at the computer and type for hours on end.

If you're serious about building a writing career, the first hurdle you have to cross is *time*. It takes time to write. It takes time to complete necessary writing-related tasks. The first thing you have to come to terms with if you want to build a writing career is that you will need to make it a priority to find time to write.

The tips and techniques I offer in this book are based on two opposite time frames. I try to give advice for those of you who don't have much time. There are seasons when I don't have much time to write, so I understand how it is. If this is you, the minimal amount of time I recommend that you commit to writing is one hour each day, five days a week. It will take longer for you to build a writing career logging in just five hours a week, but it can be done.

I also try to give advice for those of you who do have huge chunks of time each day but aren't exactly sure what to do with those hours in order to build a writing career. The maximum amount of time I recommend that you take is eight hours each day, five days a week. If you can commit to a 40-hour work-week as a writer, your career can develop quite quickly by applying the strategies I recommend. And if you're somewhere in between, you can adjust the strategies and tips to accommodate your particular time frame.

As you're getting started, keep a journal of your schedule each day. Write down what you do every single hour of your week. Then evaluate the way you're spending your time. Look for activities you can replace with writing. For instance, if you come home from work and watch TV each night, choose to sit down at the computer and write, instead. If you're busy with preschoolers from dawn to dusk each day, learn to *think* about your manuscript while interacting with them, and then grab 15 minutes to type the next section whenever a break suddenly appears. Keep a notebook and pen handy so that when you think of a perfect line, you can write it down before you forget. Every minute counts. Get up half an hour earlier each morning and stay up half an hour later each night to write. Don't answer e-mail until after you type for at least one hour each day.

If you're serious about building a writing career, the second hurdle you have to cross is *work*.

Many writers only want to write what they want to write. This is fine if you want to have a hobby. You can afford to take the time to write your manuscript from beginning to end, take it to your critique group for a number of months until it is polished to perfection, and then try to find an agent to represent you, or a publisher who is interested in publishing it. The whole process can take three to five years, or even longer. You can afford to do that if you're writing as a hobby. But it's not the way a career writer works.

Think about it. If you got hired somewhere, clocked each day into work, and worked for your assigned hours, how long could you go before you expected to see a paycheck? Three to five years? I don't think so. No. You'd be working at your job, and you'd expect to get paid for it.

It's the same regarding the job of writing. Career writers don't work the same way that a writer does who is writing for a hobby and hoping he'll someday sell his manuscript. At least not writers who make their living from writing and use their writer's income to buy the groceries, pay the electric bills, and help fund their children's college tuition. They can't afford to sit around writing only what they want to write. Career writers know they have to spend their time writing what editors want in order to earn a steady income. Career writers know that earning an income from writing takes work, even if they're not particularly interested in a certain project.

That brings us to our third hurdle. The third hurdle you have to cross if you're serious about building a writing career is *income*. Developing a strategy to earn income as a children's writer is what a large portion of this book is all about. For starters, though, read the next section. It will help you understand more about the financial aspects of writing for kids.

Beginner's Tip

It's perfectly fine to write for a hobby. Writing is my favorite hobby. If you're not ready yet to start your career, you can still implement many of these strategies into your life as a writer. Then, when you reach the day when you're ready to launch your career, you'll already be halfway there.

Professional Track

Try to network with career writers who actually make a living writing for children. Ask these adventurous souls what works for them to add up to a successful career.

1.5 Budgets and Bills

If you're looking for a job, it's probably because you need money to pay your bills. If you're hoping to build a career as a children's writer, it's probably for the same reason. It's time to take a reality check. Writing is not an "I-can-start-tomorrow-and-get-a-paycheck-next-week" kind of job. It takes time to build a reliable income. However, there are key strategies you can use to build a successful writing career and start earning income.

Unlike careers where you get hired and immediately start earning a predictable salary, a career in writing is more like a career in sales. Income depends on the sales you make.

If you need a steady salary and want to earn it immediately through writing, it's best to land a job with a publishing house or agency as an editor, assistant, copy editor, proofreader, publicist, etc. With the advancement of technology, many of these jobs can be found nowadays where you can work out of your own home. I've worked with various editors who live in an entirely different state from where their publishing house is located. They operate mainly over e-mail, hold virtual meetings with their editorial teammates via the Internet, and can quickly be reached anytime, anywhere on their cell phones.

If you already have a career but want to switch to a career in writing, keep your day job while you make the transition. Also, because writing, just like a career in sales, can bring in a huge income one year and see a large drop the next, it's best to have a nest egg stashed away for when you make the final leap. Just in case.

If it's not essential for you to start earning a sizable income right away in order to balance your budget and pay your bills, you have a little more flexibility and a lot more options to choose from.

While you're starting to build your career as a children's writer, you can earn an initial income by working at any number of various writing-related jobs. From working as an editor for a manuscript critique service to performing literature-related activities at school assemblies, there are countless opportunities to earn cash. If you want to earn the big bucks, you can even tap into the lucrative world of business writing. Check out Robert W. Bly's amazing book, *Secrets of a Freelance Writer: How to Make $100,000 a Year or More.*

For a frame of reference as you launch your writing career, study the list of fees to charge as found in the current *Writer's Market* by Writer's Digest Books. Just for starters, here are some numbers to consider:

- Many children's book publishers offer between a $1000 and $5000 advance with 5-7% royalties. Most of these publishers pay half the advance when you sign the contract and half when you submit the completed book manuscript. After the book is published, which can take a process of up to three years, the book must sell enough copies to earn the advance. After that, you start to get paid royalties. Royalty checks from many publishers are paid twice a year. Usually in April and October.

- Smaller children's book publishers might offer a 5-7% royalty, but no advance. After a manuscript is published, you start to earn royalties on the first copies that sell. You'll get your first check about six months after the royalty cycle kicks in—either April or the following October.

- Work-for-hire publishers for many children's books offer a flat, one-time payment between $1000 and $5000. This is usually paid 30 days after the completed manuscript is submitted.

- A fairly good-paying assignment for a children's magazine story or article can be between $200 and $500.

- Of course, there will be publishers who offer less than these amounts. Some publishers don't pay anything at all. And the huge publishing houses can offer an advance of $40,000 with 10% royalties to an author for a picture book they predict will sell. You hear of even more lucrative deals with MG (middle grade) or YA (young adult) novels. Most of those big publishers require agented submissions, however, or work with already established and well-known writers.

With these figures in mind, you can see that it is possible to earn an income as a children's writer. Hopefully, using the strategies found in this book, you can even start earning income this year. Read the following section to find out more.

Beginner's Tip

If you are in a financially secure place where you have time to launch a career in writing, don't feel as if you have to find work elsewhere first. Use the tips and techniques found here to get started by doing what you want to do the most: write for children.

Professional Track

If you've got published credits, many community colleges or universities might hire you to teach a course of writing. In this career, experience counts just as much as a degree—sometimes even more.

Chapter 2
Yes! You Can—but if You Feel You Can't

2.1 Learn Needed Skills

As you've been reading this book, you might have a sinking feeling growing in the pit of your stomach. Perhaps you never had a teacher who taught grammar and punctuation rules in school. Or maybe you did, but can't remember what she said. Perhaps English isn't your native language. It could be that you don't even know the basics such as how to tell the difference between a noun and a verb. Don't despair! You can learn the needed skills to become a professional writer and build a successful career. Really!

The easiest way to start learning is to go back to square one. Walk into a teacher supply store or find one online. Look for workbooks kids use in elementary school that teach writing skills. Some of my favorite books I like to recommend to writers include a set by Karen Kellaher called *Writing Skills Made Fun* (Scholastic). There are three titles: *Capitalization, Punctuation, and Spelling; Parts of Speech;* and *Sentences and Paragraphs.* Purchase all three. Then have fun. Do the puzzles. Make the manipulatives. Laugh at the silly kid jokes. And learn the basics. Yes! You can do it!

You can also learn from the pros. Study the techniques writers use in books that are already published in the genre you want to write. Purchase a user-friendly writer's guide such as *Write Right!* by Jan Venolia, and study it until you wear out the pages.

Get plugged into a critique group. A writers' group can help you improve your skills meeting after meeting. Take your current manuscript and take it back again until it's polished so it shines. But don't just rely on fellow writers to carry you through with their knowledge of basic writing skills. Make every effort you can to learn them yourself, too.

Go back to school. Many community colleges offer English classes where you can learn the basics and get helpful feedback by a trained instructor. Make this important investment now to learn the skills you need to build a successful writing career.

Once you have the basic language skills every writer needs to succeed, you still might not feel ready to launch your career. In the next section, find out how you can boost your self-esteem in a very practical way.

Beginner's Tip

Look on the Internet for an online English class that teaches pre-college basics. Sign up and learn needed skills in the comfort of your very own home.

Professional Track

Hire someone to fill in for your weaknesses. Can't type? Write in longhand and hire a typist. Got dyslexia? Write your manuscript and hire a proofreader.

Don't have time for thorough research? Write your story and hire a researcher to give you the facts.

2.2 Get Published

As a writer, one of the best ways to boost your self-esteem is to start small. Take little steps, one after the other. Just put one foot in front of the other, step by step. Soon you'll be racing down the runway, and before you know it, you'll be flying up, up, up as you reach for the sky.

The best way to start is to work on the goal to get published. Find a publisher to write for in the no-pay/low-pay market. Search locally in places such as your church newsletter or your community newspaper. Browse through your market guide and look for magazine publishers, Sunday School take-home papers, curriculum publishers and other small publishers who need lots of written material but can't afford to pay their authors much, if anything at all. Explore the Internet and look for online e-news, e-zines, and other venues that publish frequent informationals but don't offer any monetary compensation for their writers.

Choose one of these publishers to target. Study their articles and look for something that interests you. See if they have writers' guidelines or submissions guidelines for you to follow. If not, simply copy the format and word length of something they've already published. Try your hand at writing an article just for their publication. Then submit it.

If you receive a rejection, don't despair. Go back to where you started and find a different publisher to target. Write a new article for this one and submit it. Keep this cycle continuing until you receive an acceptance and notification that your manuscript will be published. Now repeat the process until you're writing manuscripts and getting published on a steady and frequent basis.

When I first launched into the children's market, I felt scared to even try to write anything at all. I didn't know anything about story arc or setting or creating characters with kid-appeal. But as I read through various children's magazines, I did notice one thing: Many featured a puzzle. I thought, "I can try this!"

Talk about starting small. I wrote a simple search-for-the-word puzzle. Then I submitted it. It was rejected. So I tried a different children's magazine. I wrote a different puzzle for them. It was accepted. So I wrote another puzzle and tried again. It was accepted again.

After about 100 more puzzles that I wrote and got published, suddenly I realized, "Hey! Maybe I could try to write a book of children's puzzles?!" My self-esteem as a writer was stronger because I'd actually been seeing a small measure of success. I contacted a publisher who published puzzle books for children and pitched an idea to write a puzzle book. Hip, hip, hooray! I landed the contract and wrote the book.

Yes, it was scary. But by then, I felt I could actually accomplish what had once seemed impossible. Getting published with small publishers frequently in one genre gave me the boost of self-esteem I needed to dare to take on the challenge of a book deadline.

Perhaps you're already getting published in the no-pay/low-pay market. You still might feel nervous about jumping into the unknown zone of writing an entire book. If you're still not sure you can do what it takes, read the next section. I'll offer practical advice on how to increase your confidence so you know you can.

Beginner's Tip

As you look for publishers to target in the no-pay/low-pay market, try to zone into the topics that interest you most at this time. It will help motivate you if you're writing about something you already love.

Professional Track

If you've already been published in periodicals in one specific genre or on one specific topic, make today the day you take that jump into hyperspace. Contact a book publisher or high-paying periodical who publishes in that exact same field of interest. List your published credits in your query and offer three to five fresh new ideas for a potential book or article. Ask if they'd like to receive a proposal for any of those ideas. Go ahead. You can do it!

2.3 *Gain Confidence*

You kinda sorta maybe think you might be able to write a manuscript from beginning to end and perhaps even after you sign a contract and have a scheduled deadline. But you're just not sure. It's this lack of confidence that's holding you back from trying. I understand. I still feel that way today. And when I do, there's something very practical I do about it. You can do it, too. This exercise will help you gain the confidence you need so you can contact editors, start landing contracts, and begin writing for deadlines.

First, think about the potential book or high-paying article assignment you'd like to write but are too scared to start. For instance, a couple of years ago, I wanted to start writing middle grade novels. I had never written a middle-grade novel before, however, and the thought of writing for this market frightened me. A million questions flew around in my mind. What if I couldn't write for that age level? What if I didn't have the stamina to write for that word count? What if I couldn't write fast enough to meet an editor's deadline? What if...?

I determined to explore my skills and interest-level as a potential writer for this genre. I made it my goal to write three entire middle grade novels and *then* determine if I was ready to try to write for this market. So I did.

I made some important discoveries along the way. I found out that it took me about a year to write each manuscript. (I used the time each week allotted to meeting my goal for personal fulfillment so that I was earning income and getting published frequently during this year with other manuscripts.) I received positive feedback from my critique group. I realized that I enjoyed writing for this age level. I discovered I could kinda sorta actually factually do it.

And so, three years later and with three complete middle grade novels under my belt, I sent off a query to a publisher of middle grade novels. I pitched a brand new idea that fit into their product line...and landed a four-book deal to write a brand new series. When we discussed deadlines for the contract, I was up front. I said that it would take me one year to write each book. (Remember how this was one of the things I discovered about myself through the process?) "No problem," the publisher replied. And I was on my way.

So how about it? Do you have an idea for a potential book or article assignment but feel too scared to try to write it? Make it your goal to explore your skills and interest-level as a potential writer for this genre. Determine to spend time writing several complete manuscripts to discover whether or not this genre is for you. If, after you complete your adventure and discover that you do feel confident enough to try, then go ahead! Start connecting with publishers. By this point, you know you can.

Beginner's Tip

On your journey of self-discovery, be honest with yourself. If you discover a certain genre isn't a good fit, try something else instead.

Professional Track

Another option is to land a contract with a small publisher in a new market you've never yet written for. A small publisher will usually be willing to work with you based on your previous track record and can offer helpful feedback and guidance along the way.

Chapter 3
Your Office

3.1 Hi-Tech Tools

To establish a career as a writer for children, there are essential hi-tech tools you must have. The good news is that if you're on a tight budget, many of these same tools are available for free. It just takes careful planning and a creative strategy to take advantage of the low-cost opportunities available. Whether you're already current on technology, or don't yet have a single item of your own, however, you can create an office space for yourself as a writer that is functional and up-to-date without going deeply in debt before you even get started.

The most basic tool every writer must have in today's hi-tech society is a working computer. A printer is essential. It's also important to have a current word-processing program. Microsoft Word is the standard in the industry. And since most editors work mainly over e-mail, you must have e-mail.

If you don't have a computer, printer, current version of Microsoft Word, or e-mail, venues like the public library are the place to go. Take a CD along to copy your files. Then set up a free online e-mail account that you can check each time you visit, and you're ready to start. However, in order to establish a successful career, make it your goal to acquire each tool.

Computer

In my circle of writer groups and writer friends, a percentage of new writers don't yet have a computer. At first, they don't want to purchase their own computer. These include the newly married, or the young mom whose husband has a computer at work but who doesn't yet have a computer at home. Also, singles who are using every penny to make ends meet sometimes don't yet have a budget for a computer. Many have had a computer at some time in their past and are computer savvy, but it crashed or became damaged in some way. Others who don't yet have a computer are hesitant to purchase one because their grandchildren have computers at their house. They either hire someone to put their handwritten manuscripts on a computer or have their grandkids do it.

If you're serious about building a career as a children's writer, however, it's paramount that you have your own computer. It needs to be your top priority. Start saving today. Look for a great deal within your budget. You'd be surprised at the fantastic sales you might find. Check out bargains on eBay, but weigh your options to include how one advantage of buying a new computer is that there usually is a warranty including technical support which might not come with a refurbished or used computer.

Be sure to purchase virus protection, or your new investment will crash and be unusable before you know it.

If Internet isn't an option yet on your budget, purchase a laptop with wireless capabilities so you can use the Internet in public places on someone else's dime.

Printer

Many stores have sales where you can get a printer for free after rebates. (Check to see if you need to purchase any necessary cables or plugs.)

Personally, with the volume of pages I print as a writer, I rely on my black and white laser printer/fax/copier/scanner. After years of dealing with the problems of inkjet printers, I finally purchased the most inexpensive laser printer I could find. It was a great deal and very affordable. It's the best investment I ever made. Inkjet printers just can't handle the volume of pages I print on a regular basis. They would always tend to break—just when my deadline was looming. And long before they absolutely died, my inkjet printers would turn out smeary pages that looked totally unprofessional.

So now, on my laser printer, I print out clean, crisp manuscript pages every time. And the fax/copier/scanner are used frequently as well for various business issues.

I also have a color all-in-one inkjet printer that I got for free when I purchased my computer. I use the color inkjet as a back-up if my laser printer runs out of ink (it never breaks) or if I need to print something in color.

Microsoft Word

Plan also to save up and look for a good deal on Microsoft Word. It really is the standard in the industry, and other word-processing programs will just be too much hassle to work with on a regular basis because of their incompatibility between computers.

Some new writers I know don't want to pay for Word but plan to use the free word processor that came with their computer. These same writers ask for help when an editor responds to their manuscript submission and can't open their computer files. I tell them they need to save up and purchase Word. Sometimes when you purchase a computer, they offer a very inexpensive discount on Microsoft Office, which includes Word. Also, refurbished or used computers such as those found on eBay often already include Word. Take advantage of any opportunity you can find to purchase Microsoft Word and use it to write your manuscripts.

E-mail

There are plenty of e-mail services to choose from at a full range of prices to fit your budget. As you're planning which e-mail service to use, network with other writers and see which they prefer.

I subscribe to a free online e-mail service. This means I go online through a Web browser to retrieve my e-mail rather than store my e-mails on my computer as some services require. The benefit of having an online service is that you can e-mail your files to yourself at the end of each working day. If your computer crashes, you can always retrieve your files online from your e-mail account by using someone else's computer. It's a great way to back up your files.

An online service is also beneficial when you're traveling because you can access your online e-mail and keep in touch with your editors from any computer you use.

Digital Camera

Another hi-tech tool you might want to add to your office is a quality digital camera. As a children's writer, there are multiple uses for a digital camera. If you're writing a craft project, the editor might want photos of each step.

If you're writing a nonfiction book or article about a place you visited, some publishers will pay for use of your photographs.

A digital camera even comes in handy when you're writing fiction. You can take photos of friends and family members as models of your characters. Or, you can photograph yourself in different poses, settings, or actions that your own characters will be in, and use these for a reference as you're writing.

And of course, if you have a blog (originally referred to as a "Web log") to help market yourself as a writer, there are a million and one opportunities to use photographs such as of book signings or special events.

Most digital cameras come with a user-friendly instruction booklet and USB cable so that you can plug your camera directly into a USB port on your computer. It's only a matter of minutes to transfer an entire photo session onto your computer where your pictures are then available for e-mail, blogs, or other uses.

Now that you know the basic hi-tech tools you'll need as a children's writer, you're ready to set up your own personal office space. Turn to the next section to find out more.

Beginner's Tip

If you're not yet computer savvy, sign up for a basic course on computers at your local library, community center, or community college.

> ## *Professional Track*
>
> For tax purposes, be sure to keep a record of each business-related purchase you make, along with receipts.

3.2 *Your Personal Office Space*

You're a writer. Isn't that exciting? Oh, you don't need to have anything published yet to call yourself a writer. And you definitely don't need to be famous. You just *are* a writer. You have that yearning and that burning to put your thoughts, ideas, and words down on a piece of paper. You have that writer's heart. So hip, hip, hooray! You're an actual factual honest-to-goodness writer. From now on you can call yourself a writer. Go ahead and tell other people you're a writer because *you* are a writer.

An essential ingredient that's important to help you feel like the writer that you are and allow you to shape your dreams into reality is to create your very own personal office space. If you don't yet have your very own office space, today is the day to start.

Your office space can be portable: a laptop computer and a tote-bag of supplies that you carry with you when you plan to take time to write. Your office space can be flexible: a card-table that fits in the corner of your bedroom during weekends and holidays, then moves to the family room during the week. Your office space can be small: a computer and printer tucked into the corner of your kitchen. It can be a small desk in your bedroom. Or, your office space can be an entire room filled with hi-tech tools, bookshelves of research books, file cabinets stuffed with manuscripts, and a customized desk just for you.

Whichever best suits your life-style, budget, or work habits, the important thing is to personalize your office space. Make it yours. Make it a comfortable, ergonomic place to come to write. You can do this in a variety of ways. You can find a personalized tote-bag if your office is portable. You can decorate your space with stickers or pictures themed with your current writing project, inspirational quotes, and stuffed mascots. Even having fancy paper to print out deadlines or using a novelty pen can help you feel like this space is yours.

Another important thing to do is make sure your office space is healthy. Good lighting is essential to reduce eye strain. Good posture is imperative for a healthy back and body, so be sure you sit in a chair that fits your size and is good for your back, even if you're using a portable laptop to write at the local coffee shop. Use a keyboard and mouse that encourage healthy hand positions to avoid developing carpal tunnel syndrome. Purchase gel wrist rests for your mouse and keyboard, or use wrist braces if necessary. By planning ahead to create an office space that encourages good health now, you'll appreciate it in the long run.

It's also helpful to have a well-stocked and organized office space. Get organized from the get-go and your life as a writer will be so much more productive. File folders, pocket folders, notebooks, paper supplies, ink and toner, staples, paper clips, pens, blank CDs to back-up your files, and sticky notes are just some of the supplies that make the writer's life so much easier when kept on hand. If you're on a limited budget, ask for these supplies for birthday gifts. Many office supply stores offer perks or rewards. Sign up for these. When you earn extra cash from purchasing necessary supplies, use the money to keep your office well-stocked with all the extras.

One more note: many writers get their best ideas in the middle of the night. If you're one of these, be sure to set up a mini-office space for those midnight muses. The famous Revolutionary Era poet, Phillis Wheatley, kept a candle, bottle of ink, and a quill pen next to her bed. Today, I keep a flashlight pen and notepad next to mine. If I wake up and suddenly solve the glitch I had been struggling with that morning, I reach for my special pen, turn on the little nightlight, and jot down my idea. Then I can go back to sleep and not worry I'll forget everything by morning.

After you set up your office space, it's important to set up a separate center for research. Read the next section to find out more.

Beginner's Tip

If you're sharing your computer with the family, set firm, but kind, limits. Make sure your family realizes this is your budding profession and respects it as such. Don't allow high-powered games that mess up your writing project or e-mail. Schedule time for each of you to use the computer. If it's too huge of a struggle to share, work with your kids to earn money to save up for their own system that can handle their really big games without crashing your word processing program. Always back up your current files each day.

Professional Track

If you're writing long hours each day, make sure you get up and move around every hour or so to take a break from your office space. To reduce stiffness or body fatigue from sitting in one place too long, take a brisk and quick walk every so often just to get a drink of water. To reduce eyestrain from staring at the computer too long, take a break, sit in a comfy chair, and write longhand for an hour. Then go back to the computer and type it in.

3.3 Research Center

A research center can be an invaluable part of your office space. It saves you time, energy, and thought by having your key research books close at hand. Whether you have a portable office, a small office, or an entire room, you can set up a successful and fully functional research center to help meet your writing needs.

I always like to create a research center for every single project that I write. Sometimes I don't need many resources and they all fit on one shelf of the bookcase I have next to my computer. When I start a new project, I clear off that shelf and put all my research books on it to have close at hand.

Sometimes I'm working on a short manuscript project, and my research center fits inside a tote-bag. This keeps my research sources handy and in one place for easy reference while I write.

Sometimes I need a lot of resources but might only have a limited amount of space. At these times, I set up a card-table and set out all my research books to organize and use as needed.

At other times, my book project has required so many research materials that I've taken over the dining table for a short period of time.

For a couple of book projects, I had the luxury of using an entire separate room for my research center, complete with its own computer desk and laptop, separate from the computer I used to type my manuscript. This was luxury indeed, but absolutely essential for projects such as the year-long nonfiction manuscript I wrote, *America's Black Founders: Revolutionary Heroes and Early Leaders with 21 Activities* (Chicago Review Press, 2009).

In my research room, I set up a laptop on the keyboard tray of my computer desk. On the desktop, I placed a small and large wooden Bookchair—one to the left of my laptop screen and one to the right of the laptop screen. The small one held a paperback book and the larger one held a larger book. I used this set-up to read and type notes directly onto my outline on the laptop. Because the books were at an exact level next to the laptop screen, there was minimal eye-strain. I could then put my updated outline on a flash drive and take it into my desktop computer in my office where I was doing the actual typing of the manuscript.

There were several reasons why I adopted this system. One reason was to reduce eyestrain and stiffness. By sitting in two different chairs staring at two different computers while working such long hours each day, it helped with both. Also, since there were so many research books to use for the entire project, my office didn't have enough room to set up my research center. The separate room was ideal.

On the rest of the desktop in my research center were my key research books for the current section of the book I was writing. In the room were book-shelves holding all my research books for the entire project—over a hundred hefty university-level volumes as well as numerous children's books. It was amazing how often I had to go back and forth between all the various books. Having them at my fingertips made my job so much easier both mentally and physically.

Whatever current manuscript project you're working on, create a research center dovetailed to meet your needs. It will make your writing task a less stressful and more productive experience. Once you have, you're ready to build your own personal research library. In the next section, I'll explain how.

Beginner's Tip

The general rule of thumb is to use three resources for each fact you state in your manuscript. A rule to remember is: If you just use one source, it's called plagiarism. If you use three sources, it's called research.

Professional Track

To find the closest libraries that carry the research books you need, check out www.worldcat.org.

3.4 Your Personal Research Library

In my research center, I always like to keep a balance of both university-level adult books as well as children's books on the same topic. The university books help me keep my facts straight and provide solid references for my publisher. The children's books help me bring important information to a child's level of understanding.

Whether you're writing a young adult or middle grade historical novel, a nonfiction beginning reader, a fiction chapter book, or a nonfiction picture book, you can build your own personal research library to help make your manuscript stand up to the fact-check it will undergo by both editors and readers alike.

Over the course of your career, I highly recommend that you start building your own personal library of key research books. By owning your key research books, you don't have to scramble back to the library a year after submitting your manuscript when the editor requests a last minute fact-check right before the book or article goes into production. And what if the library cleared your research book off the shelf and no longer carries it? To avoid frustrating situations like this, it helps to accumulate your own personal reference library.

To help it fit your budget, always keep in mind how much you'll earn for a certain project. If a publisher pays less than $100 for your particular type of manuscript, budget $20 to spend on research books. Even if you don't get any payment for your work, you can still afford $20 with careful planning, especially because it's tax deductible.

First I like to explore the general shelves and the reference section in my local library or at a local university library. I browse through their selections and write down which titles would best suit my project. Then I go home and search for these titles on Amazon.com or AbeBooks.com. Often, many expensive titles can be found used and in good condition for under $5.00 including shipping and handling. At this rate, you can stock your research shelves with 3-4 key reference books of your own.

Other resources I add to my personal research library include books by my target publisher. I use these as references to make sure my manuscript fits my target publisher like a glove. (For more information on how to target a book publisher, see *Chapter 9: Target Books.*) I also purchase magazine subscriptions or purchase used magazines from my local library if there are periodicals that can help supply current, cutting edge information about my project. Again, I make sure these purchases fit well within my budget.

On higher paying contracts where I'm paid at least several thousand dollars, I invest up to $100 to purchase my key research books. Again, I like to purchase a balance of children's books as well as university-level books.

Children's books are so helpful for a variety of reasons. For one, they help me write a concise outline of my topic to send to the publisher. For another, many publishers like to include a list in the back of the book for suggested books that students can read. Further, children's books help me boil down the essence of my topic as I'm trying to write about that topic for kids. And finally, reading the children's books on my topic helps me find my voice so I can word the concepts just right for a child's level of understanding.

The added benefit of building your own research library is that if you land another project to write about a similar topic, you already have many of the resources you already need. This helps save both time and money—two great advantages for your writing career.

Other books you'll want to add to your office are ones essential to your success as a children's author. Read the following section to find out which titles can help you the most.

Beginner's Tip

Editors don't like writers to use the Internet as their resource for research. Even a trusted site by an influential organization can change or disappear overnight. Use books as your main resources. Then, if you want to round out your facts with the Internet, that's fine.

Professional Track

Sometimes the information you need can only be found on the Internet. If this is the case, discuss this situation with your editor to get her permission to cite it as your main source.

3.5 The Children's Writer's Bookshelf

Even if your strengths don't yet include writing for children, you can learn what it takes to build a successful career as a children's writer. By stocking writer's books and magazines on your bookshelf, reading them on a steady basis, and putting their advice into practice, you can constantly be improving your craft.

There are various writer's periodicals and e-zines, or online magazines, available today. Past issues of many periodicals can be found for bargain prices at your library's used bookstore. Each year, either for a gift for myself or on my birthday wish list, I subscribe to one writer's magazine—a different one each year. This keeps me current on what's happening in the publishing world as well as helps me improve my craft. I keep writer's magazines in several spots throughout the house where I can sit and read through them at various moments throughout the week.

Market Guides

A writer's market guide is essential for finding a publisher. Set up as a type of address book, a market guide lists the name of various publishers as well as their contact information, editors' names, and a short description of types of products they publish. There are various market guides available and most come out each year.

Writer's Market includes both the adult market and the children's market and features helpful front matter such as sample queries, a chart of standard fees and payments, and author interviews.

Children's Writer's & Illustrator's Market specializes in publishers of children's books, so it includes many publishers not listed in the more general market guides.

Book Markets for Children's Writers and *Magazine Markets for Children's Writers* are both geared for the children's specialty market as well. There are also other specialty market guides such as Sally Stuart's *Christian Writers' Market Guide*.

Because each guide is unique and offers different features, I like to have a copy of each one on my shelf. However, I only budget to purchase one title each year. This way I always have one current market guide on my bookshelf. I let the other titles go back a few years, or swap with writer friends or find more recent editions at library used bookstores for less than $1.

Manuals of Style

A manual of style is essential as you write. There are various manuals of style preferred by each different publisher, but in general, *The Chicago Manual of*

Style is the accepted standard in the industry. Once again, you can find a copy for less than $5 at a university's or library's used bookstore. Since this hefty volume can be a little tricky to read, I also like to keep several user-friendly style guides on my shelves such as *Write Right!* and *Rewrite Right!* by Jan Venolia.

Another favorite by many editors and authors is Strunk and White's *The Elements of Style.*

If you're writing for the Christian market, the standard in the industry is *The Christian Writer's Manual of Style.*

All these style guides help answer common questions that arise regarding the proper use of commas, punctuation, grammar, etc.

Reference Books

Standard reference books every writer needs on her bookshelf include a dictionary, a thesaurus, and an encyclopedia. Once again, these can often be found at bargain rates in a local thrift store or library used bookstore.

Of more specialized interest to help you as a children's writer, your bookshelf can also include the following titles. *Chase's Calendar of Events: The Day-by-Day Directory to Special Days, Weeks and Months* is a must for holiday writing.

The Timetables of History is a handy book that shows you at a glance what was happening all throughout the world during the time period you are writing about.

35000+ Baby Names by Bruce Lansky is one of the best resources I've found for using to name the characters in your manuscripts because each entry lists the country of origin and the meaning of the name.

The Complete Rhyming Dictionary by Clement Wood is a helpful tool for writing in rhyme.

Children's Writer's Word Book by Alijandra Mogilner lists words according to which grade level they are taught in school and is essential when writing beginning readers or for the educational market.

A final book I recommend that you add to your bookshelf is your very own reference book. I call mine *A Zillion Zany Zingers: Nancy's Dictionary of Wow Words, Fun Phrases, and Tips to Tickle Young Readers!* It's a notebook that I fill with all sorts of goodies.

I have a list of words to use in titles that will grab my readers such as *danger, secrets,* and *whispers.*

I have a list of potential and intriguing character names such as Mindalyn McGookin, Snooks Eaglin, Mrs. Grouch, and Mrs. Smart, all of whom are real people!

I have a list of cute sayings such as "easy-peasy," "yippee skippy," and "You're up to your ears in crocodiles!"

I have a list of actions phrases such as *tore down the hall* and *dropped down on all fours.*

I have a dictionary of fun words such as crunchy, jiggle, and pizzazz.

I also have a collection of favorite passages from children's books, credited with the author and book.

In short, my own research notebook is an ongoing collection of the best of the best words and phrases that appeal to the child within me. When I'm stuck or need a fresh idea, I turn to this book to jumpstart my creative juices. Plus, it's just plain fun.

To find out more ways to add fun and sparkle to your office space, read on. In the next section, I'll share several exciting ideas.

Beginner's Tip

Keep an eye out for select titles to add to your bookshelf. Frequent thrift stores, library used bookstores, Amazon.com, and AbeBooks.com to purchase these titles at bargain prices. Many can be found for less than $1 because new editions are published each year.

Professional Track

In your critique group each year, host a holiday party with a gift exchange for used, recycled writer's books and magazines. It's a great way to clear off your shelves as well as discover and stock up on brand new classics without busting your piggybank.

3.6 Sparkles and Fun

I hope you're having fun as a children's writer. Fun is such an important element in the lives of children, even in the midst of heartache and pain. By adding the ingredient of fun into our lives as children's writers, it helps us stay connected with our target audience. Whether you're writing for infants and toddlers, or teens and young adults, you can design your office space so that it's a fun place to work.

Often, I have to write in a quiet atmosphere. There are many times, however, when I'm doing specific tasks that music is okay in the background. At times like these, I have a selection of CDs that I like to play—kids' CDs. One of them is a CD from my childhood of Robert Louis Stevenson's *A Child's Garden of Verses* set to music. These rollicking, silly, and jubilant CDs give me the light heart and joyful attitude of a kid. I'm a better children's writer because I listen to children's music regularly.

Hats are fun for any age. They have endless possibilities to add fun to the life of a writer. Got writer's block? Make or purchase a special hat and designate it as your Writer's Hat. Put it on and wear it to break out of that rut and get in the mood for writing.

I tend to balk at the self-editing phase. So I made myself an Editor's Hat to wear when I find myself postponing this important task. I plop that floppy beach hat on my head. It's decked out with a highlighter, gluestick, red pen, and sticky note pad all attached with Velcro® to the brim. I even added a name tag to the front that says "Editor's Hat." Somehow having that silly hat on my head helps add fun to an otherwise mundane task.

Next to my desk I keep some of my very favorite childhood books. On days I find myself tired of wading through the doldrums of writing, I reach for one of those books, take a moment to reconnect with the reason why I want to write children's books in the first place, and then I'm ready to get back to work.

What can you add to your office space to help you have more fun? Crayons to use while you edit? Art supplies to color a picture, cut and glue, and help you feel more connected to the world of a child? A little mascot to cheer your day? A silly little pencil holder? By adding fun little sparkles to your office space, you make sure it's a fun place to come to, sit down and stay awhile, and spend time writing.

Beginner's Tip

There's nothing quite like children's artwork to add fun to any setting. Read your story to a child. Then ask her to draw a picture about it to hang near your desk.

Professional Track

If the word "deadline" puts dread in your heart, call them "opportunities" instead. Write out a list of each of your "opportunities" on a sheet of fun specialty paper and post it in a prominent place on your desk.

Chapter 4
Critique Groups

4.1 The Joy of Community

A critique group is a community of writers who meet together to offer constructive feedback on each other's manuscripts. Each group is different and is as unique as the delicate design on a butterfly's wings. Learn to value and appreciate a critique group for what it is, and you can soar even higher to follow your dreams of building a successful career as a children's writer.

Critique groups can be large or small. Some critique groups of just three or four members thrive for years with these writers usually becoming loyal friends. Other critique groups have several hundred members and break into small groups during the critique sessions. Other critique groups fluctuate between five and twenty members at a meeting and are flexible to either meet as a whole or divide into small groups, depending upon how many are in attendance.

The format or structure of a critique group meeting can be quite diverse. Some critique groups focus their entire meeting on feedback of manuscripts. Others divide their time into different activities such as discussing market news, sharing personal success stories, and workshop presentations or guest speakers. Some even function more as a general writers' group and encourage manuscript exchanges to take place outside of the meeting. One group might have a leader and another group might have members take turns leading the discussions.

Membership in critique groups varies according to each group's focus or guidelines. Some groups comprise writers all at the same level of expertise. Others are open to writers of all levels, including beginners and professionals. Some prefer to only target one genre or format such as picture books or young adult novels. Others are open to members bringing manuscripts of every kind. In short, each critique group is its own unique community.

If you're not yet a member of a critique group, start your own and set your own guidelines to follow. Or look around for one that best suits your own personal needs and interests. There are various places to look in your search. The Society of Children's Book Writers & Illustrators at www.scbwi.org often lists local groups if you search under regional information. Sally Stuart's *Christian Writers' Market Guide* lists critique groups by state. Organizations such as the Institute of Children's Literature and the Christian Writers Fellowship International often post information in their e-news or online forums. You can also ask at your public library or local writer's conferences for information on groups that might meet in your area or online. I highly recommend every writer join a critique group.

There are many important reasons to discover the joys of joining a community of writers. For one, it gives valuable and consistent feedback on practical ways to improve your manuscripts and thus your writing skills. Sharing your manuscript with others also helps prepare you for that eventful day when you submit it for an editor to consider. If the editor offers suggestions for improvement, your feelings won't be hurt that she didn't absolutely love your "baby" because you're already used to making revisions based on other people's feedback. Another reason it's important to join a critique group is because of the many opportunities for networking.

Even if joining a group sounds intimidating at first, take the step and sign up. You'll quickly make friends and find the support you need. To learn about getting the most out of the critique group you join, read the next section.

Beginner's Tip

If your critique group comprises only beginning writers, start each meeting by reading a how-to-write article written by a professional, published writer.

Professional Track

If you've had a bad experience with critique groups in the past, don't avoid critique groups any longer. Discover the joy of a writer's community. Form a small critique group comprising hand-picked published writers in your genre to provide professional feedback uniquely suited to your personality, needs, and interests.

4.2 Self-Editing Strategies

A critique group is a wonderful place to be involved as a writer. A group's helpful and constructive feedback can bring the quality of your manuscript up a notch. If you quickly type out the first draft of your manuscript the morning of your meeting, however, your group will have to spend the session attending to basic grammar and punctuation mistakes. Why not learn to self-edit your manuscript first, *before* you bring it to your group? With Level 1 being the best a manuscript can be, instead of just bringing it from a Level 5 to a Level 4, your group can now help you bring it up from a Level 3 to a Level 2. Here are specific techniques to incorporate into your own self-editing sessions so you can get the most out of your critique group's input.

Check the basics. Read over your manuscript, checking grammar and mechanics such as punctuation usage, sentence structure, and spelling. If the task seems daunting, start small and edit one paragraph, short section, or page. Use a highlighter to mark mistakes, weaknesses, and awkward spots. Not sure what to look for? Use Jan Venolia's *Rewrite Right!* to make your own checklist of items to spot.

Review the sequence. In nonfiction, does your manuscript progress from Point A to Point Z in a logical order? In fiction, do scenes develop and work together to move the plot forward in an effective and logical way?

Edit for genre-specific strengths and weaknesses. In nonfiction, does your tone suit your readership? Is it academic, preachy, or conversational? Does your manuscript reach a satisfying and sensible conclusion? In fiction, have you adequately developed your characters, plot, dialogue, conflict, and scenes?

Each genre has its own attributes to focus on. Find several how-to books pertaining to writing in your genre. Make a check-off list of key elements to self-edit. Go through your manuscript before you take it to your next critique group meeting and work to self-edit the pages as best as you know how at this point of your career.

As you're working to improve your self-editing skills, you can also learn how to be a vital, successful member of your group. Read the next section to find out more.

Beginner's Tip

If you've never learned the basic grammar and punctuation rules in school, don't despair. Find an elementary student's skills book online or in a teacher supply store and complete the exercises yourself to sharpen your skills. Recommended books include these three titles by Karen Kellaher, published by Scholastic Teaching Resources:

- *Writing Skills Made Fun: Capitalization, Punctuation, and Spelling*

- *Writing Skills Made Fun: Parts of Speech*
- *Writing Skills Made Fun: Sentences and Paragraphs*

> ### *Professional Track*

Work with your group to develop a check-off list for self-editing strategies that all members can use before they bring their manuscripts to the group.

4.3 Be a Successful Member

Just as any group can only be as successful as its members, make it your goal to become a valuable member of your critique group. Whether you're the leader of the group or its newest member, you can influence your group in powerful, positive ways.

Be Encouraging

Writing is an often lonely and discouraging occupation. We writers frequently face numerous painful rejections long before we ever get one iota of validation. A critique group should therefore be a place of encouragement, a place where we feel validated as writers, and a place where we get the strength to carry on. Make it your goal to speak encouragement into the hearts and souls of your fellow writers. Write encouraging notes on the manuscripts you critique. Even with the most poorly written manuscript, look for ways to give positive feedback such as "I can tell writing this section meant a lot to you." We all have to start at square one. Make it your job to encourage each other to rise to the next step.

Be Constructive

It's easy to grab our red pen and write vague, discouraging comments in large letters such as "This passage does nothing for the manuscript." Before we comment on our fellow member's manuscript, however, let's give careful thought to how we can word our comment in a more positive, specific, and constructive way. For instance, we could write, "The following paragraph supports your topic. Move it up here to replace this one."

Be Courteous

Follow the rules set up by your critique group. Stay within time restraints, page count, and genre. Let others speak first and try not to dominate the conversations. Listen and learn to value other members' feedback even if you disagree. When your own manuscript is under the magnifying glass, graciously accept suggestions and feedback without arguing your defense. After you go home, it's your choice as the author whether or not to plug those suggestions into your manuscript. During the critique session, however, it's best to be gracious and appreciative of everyone's perspective.

Be Sensitive

If your manuscript covers controversial, dark, or edgy territory, be aware that some members may not care to read it. Be up-front and politely ask members if your material is within their comfort zone. If it's not, be gracious and accommodating. Either omit certain potentially offensive passages when you bring your manuscript to the group, or bring an entirely different body of work instead. Connect with specific members on the side who are willing to exchange feedback outside of group time.

Be Fair

Often a critique group simply doesn't offer enough time to cover all the pages that you need to bring. With the leader's permission, the proper etiquette is to send an e-mail to all members of your group and ask if anyone might have the time or interest to exchange longer or extra manuscripts for critique outside of group time. This avoids the awkward situation of asking a specific member who might have to turn you down because of personal or time restraints. It also opens the gate for an *exchange* so that you are giving others an opportunity for receiving feedback on their manuscript in exchange for editing your own. This helps members feel like they're not being taken advantage of, especially if they're published writers and are constantly getting bombarded with people asking for free critiques.

Be Enthusiastic

Make it your goal to be part of your group in every way possible. If your group wants to start a blog, jump on board with enthusiasm. If your group plans to self-publish a writers' how-to book, sign up to submit material. If your group hosts a contest each year, volunteer as a judge. Don't be a nay-sayer and vote down creative ideas the members want to do as a group. If these activities just aren't your cup of tea, find another group. If you value this group enough to continue as a member, be enthusiastic about other members' ideas, and join the fun.

Be Professional

People are giving up valuable time and energy to attend your critique group. Make your group count. Learn how editors and publishers edit manuscripts and make it your goal to do the same. *The Chicago Manual of Style* lists the standard in the industry for proofreaders' marks. Photocopy those pages and use the same notations when you edit. Study a manual of style to learn the correct terms to use when identifying certain weaknesses such as dangling participle, incorrect verb tense, and inconsistent point of view. Always be reading a writer's how-to book, a writer's magazine, and a book focused on your current genre. Work hard to be a professional writer as well as a professional member of your critique group.

Sometimes, a critique group can get stuck in a rut. Or, a group might not quite meet all your current needs as a writer. If you want to give a new face-lift to your critique group, or even want to start your own, read the next section to find out more.

Beginner's Tip

Not all manuals of style are the same. Even though the basic content is the same, some are much more user-friendly than others. Browse through your local library or bookstore to find one that fits your comfort zone.

Professional Track

To help your critique group members be on the same level of expertise when editing, hand out a welcome pack to new members that includes a copy of proofreaders' marks, as well as a suggested style guide that your members have adopted to use.

4.4 *Organize an Open Membership Group*

If you're not yet a member of a critique group, or if you want to help your current critique group get a brand new look and feel, here are ideas to help you get started. It's amazing the things you can do that are simple, yet effective, to produce and shape the critique group of your dreams.

Over the years, I've been part of a variety of critique groups. Most of them I've formed on my own. One of my favorites, however, is the open membership critique group. Open genre, open number of members, and open to all levels of expertise. This kind of a critique group is always growing and changing as new members join the ranks. It's an exciting place to be!

If you'd like to organize a brand new critique group in your area that is open to everyone, the first thing to do is find a location. Because you don't know who will attend this group, you should meet in a public place that has insurance to handle a group, such as a meeting room in the public library, a community building, a restaurant with a certain amount of privacy, or quiet corner in a large local bookstore. It should be easily accessible to members, preferably central to various local points of the compass. Next to a freeway exit is helpful. An added benefit is if there is a coffee shop or restaurant within walking distance. This comes in handy for longer meetings, whether to break in the middle for a meal or to gather afterward for lunch. This spot should handle either a small or large group with ease, depending on the number of people who join.

Once you've found a potential location, choose a name for your group. Then determine the date, frequency, and time your group will meet. Some prefer weekends, others prefer evenings, and still others, like me, prefer meeting midday in the middle of the week. As the organizer of this new group, you get to pick what works best for you.

Next, advertise your group. When I first started an open member critique group in the community where I had just moved, I asked the local paper to interview me. They ran a great story where I described my interests in writing, listed the details about the new group I was forming, and concluded with an invitation for anyone to come to the first meeting. Several people saw the article in the newspaper and showed up, along with a few friends I personally invited. Our critique group was off and running!

Before you meet for the first time, create a welcome pack to hand out to every member. On the first page, I printed the basics:

- Name of Group

- PURPOSE: To encourage writers to best meet personal writing goals as they improve their writing skills.

- WHO: Our group welcomes beginning, experienced, and published writers. All levels are invited to attend. Membership is free; there are no fees.

- WHAT: Each person brings a pencil/pen and about 6 copies of one manuscript (1-10 pages, typed and double- spaced).

- WHEN: List the day, frequency you'll meet, and time of the meeting.

- WHERE: List the address and phone number of your meeting place.

- QUESTIONS: List your name, contact phone and/or e-mail.

Within the welcome pack itself, I included a photocopy of *The Chicago Manual of Style's* Proof-readers' Marks, a one page check-off list of basic manuscript attributes to look for during the critique, and several encouraging as well as instructional articles about critique groups in general.

The logistics of an open membership group work much better if you plan to shift according to the number of members who attend each meeting. It helps to have several tables set up, each with 4-6 chairs. Over the years, I've found that a general rule of thumb is to break into small groups of four if more than eight members show up.

Twenty minutes allotted for each member is usually adequate time to read over 10 pages of a manuscript and offer constructive feedback. A timer is helpful in the hands of a volunteer timekeeper, if you find meetings or individuals take too long. Be sure to allow 15-30 minutes at some point during the meeting to discuss marketing updates, share member news, and discuss any upcoming events.

Currently, I lead an open member group called CHAIRS (Christian Authors, Illustrators, and Readers Society). You can visit our website at www.chairs7.wordpress.com for tips on organizing your own group.

CHAIRS has the first hour slotted for discussion topics such as marketing updates, beginner's tips, and member news. We invite a guest speaker to talk or present a mini-workshop during the second hour, along with a book signing if she has published books. During the third hour, we break into critique groups of two or three members each. Those who haven't brought a manuscript to critique for that meeting are divided evenly among the groups and invited to provide feedback as well.

Perhaps you already belong to an open member group and would like to be part of a closed, professional group as well. In the next section, I'll share how to organize and run a successful closed membership group.

> ## *Beginner's Tip*
>
> Your critique group can be successful even if its members are all beginning writers. Even if you don't yet know *why* a spot in a manuscript needs to be rewritten, you can still point out *where* it's awkward and needs improvement.

> ## *Professional Track*
>
> If your critique group comprises all levels of expertise, be sure to offer something for everyone. Discussing a different topic such as queries, simultaneous submissions, and point of view at each meeting will keep the newbies coming back. Inviting local published authors to speak at your meetings will keep your career writers enthusiastic as well.

4.5 Operate a Closed Membership Group

Perhaps you want to belong to a small group of writers who grow together in your craft at the same pace. You might want to be part of a critique group that focuses on one genre. Or, you might want to form a group where every member is on the same level of expertise. Whatever your reason, you can form a successful closed critique group that helps you pursue your dreams.

Before you form this group, however, it's important to plan ahead. Chat with other potential members to discuss a common ground upon which you can build your group. Choose a central location to meet. Determine if you'll feel comfortable meeting in someone's home or in a public locale.

Since this group is tightly focused, it's probably best to keep it as an invitation-only group. Make sure that each potential member understands the clear purpose of this group.

I've been a member of a closed membership group for several years called Wordsmiths. Each one of us writes for the children's market. We are all seriously committed to seeking publication for our manuscripts. This group is a highlight of my writer's life. (You can visit our blog at www.wordsmiths8.wordpress.com.)

Since our members live fairly far apart from each other, we meet at the food court of a mall centrally located and next to a freeway exit. We allot 20 minutes for each person to share up to ten pages of a typed and double-spaced manuscript. Our timekeeper uses a timer to help us keep track of time.

We break midway through our meeting for lunch together in the food court. This time doubles as the opportunity to share exciting news, encourage each other through the normal process of receiving rejections, and discuss current updates in the publishing world and marketing trends.

We limit our group membership to eight members. This keeps the meeting manageable. We meet once a month. This allows our members to participate in other critique groups with a different focus. We keep our information confidential. This frees us to share openly and honestly about circumstances we encounter as writers.

If you would like to belong to a closed group with a tight focus, but don't know other local writers with your same interests, then an online group might be your best choice. In the next section, I'll show you how to successfully set one up.

Beginner's Tip

If other writers want to join your closed group, keep their names and contact information on a waiting list. Sometimes one of your members might have to suddenly drop out. Maintaining a waiting list will help plug in a new member smoothly and quickly.

Professional Track

If you've been a member of a closed group for a long time, it might be nice to help a second, similar group get started in your area. Offer to mentor the new group by having your own members take turns visiting its meetings until they feel confident to operate on their own.

4.6 Set up an Online Group

We live in an amazing age. The Internet can connect us quickly and easily with people around the world. If you want to form a closed group that focuses on one specific genre but can't find any other local writers who share your interest, an online group could be the perfect solution.

Or, if you live far away from other writers, an online group can connect you immediately with writers from around the world.

Even if you live close to numerous writers' groups but your schedule prohibits you from joining, membership in an online group can allow you to participate during the hours that work best for you and from the comfort of your own home.

I was invited to join an online picture book critique group—and it's one of the best experiences I've ever had as a writer. We encourage each other daily through e-mails and stay current on each other's news. Whether we touch base with one another during the wee hours of the morning or midday over lunch, we each sit down at our own time and in our own space to connect. It's great! We feel like family.

If you want to start your own online critique group, the best way to advertise for members is...online! The Institute of Children's Literature hosts a place online where authors can enlist other children's writers from around the world. It's the perfect place to start. There are also countless listserves and online children's writers' forums where you can look for potential members.

There are various strategies you can use to set up your online group, but I'll share how our group works. We have eight members. Our focus is picture books, so we only critique picture book manuscripts. We voted on a name, Pens and Brushes. We appointed a moderator whose job is to post updated submissions schedules and check that all members are following the group guidelines. We set up a Yahoo group so that when we send an e-mail, it reaches our entire group at once. This increases our sense of community. We also set up a free website at www.PensAndBrushes.wordpress.com. This gives us a link to use for a reference to send editors when we submit our manuscripts. A group website shows editors we're serious about our craft. It also helped us get to know each other better because we included photos and bios for each of our members.

Here are our group guidelines:

1. Submissions will continue on an alphabetical basis based on our last names, A-Z. Because of the different computers we all have, we try to remember to submit an attached file of the manuscript as well as a copy of it pasted within the body of the e-mail in case someone can't open a file.

2. When it's your turn, please submit your manuscript to the entire group over the weekend (Saturday or Sunday). If we haven't received your manuscript by Sunday midnight, we'll look forward to receiving it the next time your turn rolls around in two months.

3. Please mark comments on the manuscript. See below for tips on how to do this.

4. E-mail manuscripts with comments to the entire group by Friday midnight of the same week.

5. Always e-mail to the entire group through our Yahoo group as much as possible to help us keep the feel of a group and a conversational style going on.

6. If you are going on vacation or have a tight deadline or get sick and can't submit a manuscript during your week, please let the moderator know as soon as possible, so she can alert the next person on the list and see if that writer might be ready with a manuscript to move forward and fill your slot. Also let the moderator know if you can't critique during a certain short period of time.

7. If you find you can't maintain the commitment of submitting one manuscript every two months and critiquing one manuscript each week, we certainly understand. Life gets busy! Just let the moderator know that you will need to step down from the group as a courtesy so that someone else on a potential waiting list can join.

8. Always remember: As in any critique group, confidentiality is a must. Please do not discuss or e-mail people's manuscripts or projects with others outside of this group.

9. Please try to keep your comments encouraging and helpful. Try to mark at least two positive comments on every single page of the manuscript even if it's just to say "I like this part!" In our business where rejections abound, a critique group can be and should be a place we find hope, encouragement, and practical help to follow our dreams.

Develop your own style and codes for critiquing. These codes are referred to as the "Crit Key." The common guidelines used are:

[DELETE] = put the portion to be deleted in square brackets in red

{ADD} = put the text to be added in the flower brackets in red

<any special comments>

(compliments can be written in green)

Whether you decide to join an existing critique group or organize a brand new one of your own, the important thing is that you are part of a critique group. It's also an added perk if your critique group is a fun place for all its members to be. To find out how to add sparkle and pizzazz to your group, read the next section.

Beginner's Tip

Perhaps you've joined an online critique group and can't keep up with the continuous pace. It can feel like you've signed up for a marathon when you've only trained for the 100-yard dash. Discuss a different submission schedule with your group, or organize or join an entirely new group that best meets your personal schedule so you don't feel as overwhelmed.

Professional Track

If you write in a specific genre and nobody else in your existing critique group does, you run the risk of having your manuscript butchered by an inexperienced eye instead of fine-tuned to perfection. It's time to form or join a genre-specific critique group where you can be confident your work will get the first-aid it deserves.

4.7 Fun, Fun, Fun!

Whether you belong to an open membership group, a closed membership group, or an online group, your critique group can be a fun place to belong. If it's not, here are some ideas to jumpstart your creativity. Let the good times roll!

Design a T-shirt for members of your group to wear. Ask members to submit various designs and then vote on your favorite. Many communities have a local printer that can make T-shirts at a reasonable price. If not, check out the numerous resources on the Internet.

A custom-designed totebag sporting your group name and logo is also a winner. Be sure to choose a bag that's wide enough to hold pocket folders and notebooks, and not too deep that your manu-scripts get lost inside. Pockets for pencils, keys, cell phone, and a water bottle are extra perks. Check online for great deals your members can afford.

A nametag badge and lanyard add extra fun, especially if the lanyard is custom designed with your website address. This is a great addition for open membership groups since nametags help members in large groups connect faster and easier. In my group, CHAIRS, we offer a welcome pack for new members to purchase at cost that includes a totebag, lanyard, nametag badge, and writing book. It's a great way to help new members feel like they belong.

Hosting annual events can add lots of energy and excitement to your group. A contest, goal, annual holiday party, or mini-retreat all help to connect your members together and increase feelings of camaraderie. In the past, my critique groups have participated in the *Periodical Challenge* (we submit to the magazine of our dreams) as well as the *Book in a Month Club* (we write an entire book manuscript from beginning to end in just one month). Join an event that's already taking place, or create your own like we did.

Hosting a blog or website also adds spark to a group. It gives individual members a common purpose as you work together to maintain the site. It also gives your group credibility with editors and publishers because it shows them your members are serious about the career of writing.

The important thing is for a critique group to be an exciting, encouraging, and helpful community. You can help make it happen.

Beginner's Tip

If your critique group is in a rut, try changing its location. Or rotate from place to place. Sometimes just changing the environment offers a fresh, new group outlook.

Professional Track

If you belong to a larger group, consider hosting a local conference each year. If you charge a fee to attend the conference, you can pay for editors as well as published authors to speak. To help you get started, chat with other writers' groups that host a conference to find out what it takes.

Chapter 5
The Triple Crown of Success

5.1 Three Separate Strategies for Three Separate Goals

Are you tired of your lack of published credits? Are you dejected over too many rejections? Do you feel like you're spinning your wheels and not making any progress at all? Don't despair! You can build a successful career as a children's writer. I'll show you how.

I call my approach the *Triple Crown of Success*. I've been using it for years to build my own career, and I'll share with you how you can use it, too. This approach brings a much lower level of frustration to me as a writer. It helps me better meet my writing goals. It makes me happy to be a writer. In short, it spells success.

Here's the super-duper, extra-special, million-dollar secret to my Triple Crown of Success:

> **Use three separate strategies to meet three separate goals.**

You see, there are three main reasons people write:

1. For personal fulfillment
2. To get published
3. To earn income

Most writers write one manuscript and try to make it meet all three goals. They get inspired to write an idea about a topic they feel passionate about. They spend a lot of time, heart, and energy writing that manuscript. Then they try to send it on its rounds of submissions to find a publisher. Deep inside, they hope it earns millions. I know. Because I've done this very thing. The end result? I won the award at a writer's conference for receiving the most rejections in one year.

I've discovered a different way. I call it the Triple Crown of Success. I have developed three entirely different strategies to use to accomplish these three separate goals. I used the Triple Crown of Success, unknowingly, when I landed my very first book contract as a raw, unskilled beginner. I use the Triple Crown of Success now with purpose to land book contracts today.

Do you want to learn how you can use this, too? Read the next section to find out more.

Beginner's Tip

Always believe in yourself. I started at square one when I knew absolutely nothing about the world of publishing. From that start, I've built a successful writing career. You can, too! Always remember: *If one can, anyone can. If two can, you can, too!*

Professional Track

Even if you already have a strategy that works for you, make it your goal to incorporate the Triple Crown of Success into your writing life to take your career to the next level. Perhaps it will even help you make that giant leap forward you've been dreaming of.

5.2 Write for Personal Fulfillment

This strategy is similar to the one you're familiar with. Write a manuscript that is near and dear to your heart. Work on it at your own pace. Take it to your critique group for feedback on how you can improve the manuscript itself and your own skills as a writer. Try to get it published if you want to share it with others. Try to sell it for a nice tidy fee if you want it to earn income.

This is the strategy you'll hear most authors and editors discuss at writers' conferences. This is the strategy you'll read about in author interviews in the top writing magazines. This is a great strategy to follow if you want to attain your goal of writing for personal fulfillment. But it won't work if you want to establish a career.

Why not? Because it can take years to find a publisher. How can you pay the bills during that time? This isn't the way to build a writing career that earns you a steady income. Instead, it's more like supporting a hobby.

If this is the only strategy you use as a writer, it can also leave you feeling as dejected as Vincent Van Gogh. Nobody purchased his paintings. In everyone's opinion, his artwork was worthless. He lived with so many rejections that he eventually committed suicide. Yet today we know his paintings are priceless. What if the same is true about your own manuscripts? What if they're meant for a different generation to appreciate fully? What if your manuscripts are well-written but get constant rejections because they're for a different time and place?

Yes, keep writing these manuscripts that you feel passionate about. Keep pursuing your goal. Just keep them under the category of writing for personal fulfillment. If you want, submit them to the top editors at the top publishing houses. Sure, if they get published, great! If they earn income, super! But don't make that your primary goal with these projects.

Here are some do's and don'ts to use as you pursue your goal of writing for personal fulfillment:

- Don't make the common mistake of lumping all your manuscripts into one general pile and trying to accomplish the three main goals with all of them.

- Do remember I recommend using a separate strategy to meet each separate goal. For every single manuscript you have already written or have even fleshed out for the idea stage, place this under writing for personal fulfillment. Writing to get published and writing to earn an income require a different strategy with brand new ideas and brand new manuscripts specifically targeted to each different potential publisher.

- Don't place too much emphasis on getting a manuscript published that you already wrote. Of course it would be fantastic if it does get published, but the publishing industry is so competitive in today's economy that you can get frustrated very, very quickly as a writer if you make it your main goal to publish or earn income from a manuscript you already wrote.

- Do remember—for manuscripts you already wrote, keep sending these out to publishers or working on them mainly for personal fulfillment. Spend time with these manuscripts to make you feel personally satisfied as a writer. But remember to set these manuscripts aside and use a different strategy to accomplish goals for getting published or earning income as a writer.

So go ahead! Write for personal fulfillment. Just be sure to use a separate strategy to get published—frequently and on a regular basis. Use an entirely separate strategy to earn income—enough so that you can actually make a living from writing. Read the next section to find out more.

Beginner's Tip

If other writers insist on telling you to follow their recommended approach to become a successful writer, ask them if they earn a steady income as a writer and get published frequently. If not, take their advice with a grain of salt.

Professional Track

If you're spending all your time writing for editors and deadlines, be sure to stop at least once each week and spend time working on a manuscript that is near and dear to your heart. This will help you avoid burnout and will connect you with your writer's heart and why you wanted to write in the first place.

5.3 Write to Get Published

Are you getting published as often as you'd like? Or has it been years since you saw your name in print? Perhaps you've not yet ever been published. No matter what your experience has been in the past, I've got exciting news for you today. If you want to build a successful writing career, you can actually take control of this seemingly elusive building block. You can get published frequently and on a steady basis. You can start today.

Always remember! The million-dollar secret to my Triple Crown of Success is to:

> ## Use three separate strategies to meet three separate goals.

For my goal to get published frequently and on a steady basis, I target the no-pay/low-pay publishers. That's right. I want to get published. So I'm specifically targeting markets that practically guarantee they'll publish my manuscripts. No-pay/low-pay markets aren't lower in *quality*. But they are lower in *quantity* of writers who submit to them. They're hungry for submissions. So when I want to get published, I target publishers who are hungry to publish my manuscripts.

How do I do this? In several ways. I look in my market guides for the publishers who pay only in copies or who offer a small compensation. I skip past those big names that everyone wants to write for. They hand out rejection letters like candy. Instead, I look for publishers that will want me to write for them.

As I search, I specifically look for publishers in the genre that interests me. I also look on the Internet for online opportunities. I look in my neighborhood and community for publications such as community magazines or church newsletters. I also look outside the box in not-so-obvious areas such as publications that need book reviews, puzzles, crafts, or fillers.

After I choose three to five publishers to target, I study their periodicals. Then I write and submit a manuscript or query to them that will fit their publication like a glove. If they reject it, I move to another publisher. If they accept it, I start communicating with their editor to determine what other types of submissions they would like to receive from me. I work with these editors until I have three to five publishers lined up throughout the year that are accepting my manuscripts and publishing them on a frequent and regular basis.

Here are some do's and don'ts to use as you pursue your goal of getting published:

- Don't try to submit manuscripts you've already written to meet this goal. Of course you want to get these manuscripts published, but put those manuscripts under writing for personal fulfillment.

- Do remember the strategy I recommend for getting published: Find three to five no-pay/low-pay publishers and write original manuscripts or queries to fit into their publication.

- Don't go for the big houses that everyone wants to get published with. These publishers hand out rejection letters like candy.

Sure, you can try to get published with them—but put that goal under writing for personal fulfillment.

- Do remember your goal is to get published frequently and on a steady basis. Look for publishers who are hungry for manuscripts because fewer writers submit to them.

- Don't be content with just one published article with a no-pay/low-pay publisher. If it felt too easy to get published there, that doesn't mean it wasn't a valuable opportunity for you as a writer.

- Do develop a relationship with the editor of the no-pay/low-pay publisher. After one manuscript is accepted, submit another to the exact same publisher...and another. This boosts morale, builds confidence, increases your list of published credits, and provides much-needed, frequent practice in the real world of writing.

It might sound strange. Why do I waste my time with the "little guys"? Because they practically guarantee me reaching my goals of getting published. I know I'll see my work in print numerous times in the year ahead. But my goal is also to earn a nice tidy income as a writer. I have a separate strategy for that. Read the next section to find out more.

Beginner's Tip

Treat every publisher you work with in a professional way, even if they don't pay. Meet deadlines on time. Submit crisp, clean manuscripts free from typos and spelling errors. You never know when an editor you work with might get promoted. If you're a great writer to work with, they might want to take you up the ladder with them.

Professional Track

Submitting manuscripts to get published frequently by the no-pay/low-pay publishers can actually help you market your books. Target periodicals or online venues that cover the same topic your book covers. Include a byline at the end of the article listing your name, your book's title, and your website or blog. It's free advertising while increasing your published credits. A win-win situation!

5.4 Write to Earn Income

It's a tough economy in our world today. It's a competitive market in the publishing industry. Yet, in spite of the odds, you can make a decent living writing for kids. You can build a successful writing career.

Always remember! The million-dollar secret to my Triple Crown of Success is to:

> ## *Use three separate strategies to meet three separate goals.*

As I plan my strategy to earn income each year, the first thing I toss out the window is my goal to write for personal fulfillment. The second thing I set aside is my goal to get published. Now I'm ready to focus on setting my goal to earn an income.

Money. Cash. Salary. That's why people get out of bed every day and go to work. That's why they stick with a job even when they don't like it. They have to pay the bills. They have to pay the rent. They have to buy groceries. So does a writer. Therefore, as a writer, I put on my job-hunting hat and look for a job that pays.

For me, this means trying to land a book contract. Other writers might land jobs writing for corporate America. (For solid advice on how to earn big bucks writing for the business world, read *Secrets of a Freelance Writer: How to Make $100,000 a Year or More* by Robert W. Bly.) Other writers might try to land a contract to write an article for a high-paying magazine. Each different venue requires a slightly different strategy, but they're still all about landing a job that pays cash.

Earning income might not necessarily be writing about something that's in your top ten fields of interest. That's okay because you're using a separate strategy to write for personal fulfillment. It might not get published for three years. That's okay because you're using a separate strategy to get published on a frequent and regular basis. But it should be something that will earn an income. That's what this strategy is all about.

Since my goal as a children's writer is to try to land a children's book contract, here is the strategy I use. I look for children's book publishers who accept queries. Many publishers don't. I skip over them for now. I look for one of the many publishers who states in their guidelines that they accept queries and have books that I say, "I think I can try to write that!"

I look for these publishers in lots of places. I look in the bookstore. I look in writer's market guides. I look in the library. I look on Amazon.com. I look in writer's magazines for interviews of book editors. I look at writer's conferences where editors come to speak.

After I find a publisher who accepts queries and has books that I think I could try to write, I study the publisher's website. I get to know their product line and then try to think of three to five topics for a new book that would fit into their product line that they haven't already done.

Then I send a query to the editor asking if she'd like to see a proposal for any of the topics on my list.

That's it.

I send out a very specific query to a publisher that I've targeted. (For more information on how to write a query, see section *13.1 Manuscript Submissions* in Chapter 13.) Then I repeat the process. I send out another query to a different publisher with a different list of topics that might fit into their product line. Then I send out another query to a different publisher with a completely different list of topics that might fit into their product line. Notice that I don't send the same list of topics to different publishers. I tailor each list to fit each different publisher. And I don't send them manuscripts I've already written. I send them queries for new topics that fit their exact product line.

I keep sending out new queries on a regular basis until I hear back from one of the editors who says, "Yes, I'd like to receive a proposal on that topic."

Then I take about a month to prepare a proposal. (For more information on how to write a proposal, see section *9.4 Contact Your Target Publisher* in Chapter 9.) As soon as that's in the mail, I go back to my initial strategy of sending out another query to a different publisher with a different list of topics. I keep doing this until I land my next book contract.

And then I write the book. *After the book contract.*

It's kind of like the old saying, "Which came first, the chicken or the egg?"

Everywhere you go, they tell you to write the book first and then try to sell it.

But that's not the strategy I use when I want to earn income. That's the strategy I use when I write for personal fulfillment. When I write to earn income, I land a contract first. And then I spend my time writing that book because I know I'm getting paid for it. It's scary, but it guarantees paying the bills.

I wrote my very first book after landing a contract, and I still do that today. Right now I'm under contract to write three books. I just finished writing a book that I signed the contract for over a year ago. I'm in the business of writing and I line up deadlines and book contracts the way a writer's organization lines up their events for the upcoming year. It works because it guarantees that I'm spending my time writing something that's already under contract. It guarantees I'll meet my goal to earn an income in the year ahead.

Here are some do's and don'ts to use as you pursue your goal of writing to earn an income:

- Don't list manuscripts you've already written as a strategy to accomplish this goal. Of course you want to earn income from what you've already written, but put those manuscripts under writing for personal fulfillment.

- Do remember the strategy I recommend for earning income: submitting well-targeted queries to editors about ideas that fit into their product line.

- Don't aim for a vague goal that you want to try to earn income in the year ahead.

- Do write down a specific goal such as: I will subscribe to the *Children's Writer*. Each month, I will choose one editor they interviewed in their articles. I will study that publisher's Web page, look at their product list, and send that editor a query listing three to five potential topics that fit into their books. In the query, I'll ask them if they'd like to see a proposal on any of those topics. Say to yourself, "My goal is to send out one query each month following this strategy."

- Don't write the manuscript first and then try to submit it to earn an income. Put that under writing for personal fulfillment.

- Do try to land a contract before you write the manuscript. This guarantees you're spending your valuable writing time actually getting paid.

Beginner's Tip

Do you feel scared that you aren't qualified to write a manuscript under contract? Get your writing muscles in shape by getting published frequently with no-pay/low-pay publishers. It's a great way to build your confidence.

Professional Track

Try to target a balance of work-for-hire publishers as well as royalty publishers each year. Work-for-hire publishers pay cash up-front for quick deadlines.

Royalty publishers promise a potential solid base of income spread out over several upcoming years.

Chapter 6
The Writer's Pyramid

6.1 Building the Pyramid

Building a successful writing career is like building a pyramid. First, you start at the bottom and build a strong base. Then you build upon your firm foundation, up...up...up...as if you are reaching for the stars. By following this basic principle, you can take practical steps to establish yourself as a professional writer, build a successful career, and see your dreams become a reality. I'll show you how.

The *Writer's Pyramid* is a model to use if you haven't yet been published very much. It's also a model I recommend for you to use if you have been published a lot but can't seem to make that jump into the next level of your career.

It's a model I've developed over time that is based on what works for me as a writer. It's a model I still use today. I've shared key concepts about the Writer's Pyramid with others, too, and those who implement this model into their own schedule see valuable results.

Writer's Pyramid #1—Before a Contract

To visualize this model, draw a triangle on a piece of paper. Draw two horizontal lines across the inside of the triangle so that it is divided into thirds. There is a large section at the base of the triangle, a medium-sized section in the middle, and a small section on top.

- Label the bottom section: No-pay/low-pay markets.

- Label the middle section: Income.

- Label the top section: Personal fulfillment.

The Writer's Pyramid works hand-in-hand with the Triple Crown of Success (using three separate strategies to meet three separate goals). In essence, the Writer's Pyramid helps you manage your time and focus your energies on very specific purposes each day in your writing week as you pursue the Triple Crown of Success.

If you want to build a solid writing career, I recommend starting with the bottom section. Begin to build your Writer's Pyramid by spending a major part of your writing efforts each week writing manuscripts for the no-pay/low-pay periodical markets. This forms the firm foundation your career needs to succeed. Why? It keeps you writing for three to five different editors at a steady basis. This builds your writing skills and boosts your confidence. It keeps you getting published frequently and regularly. This validates your writer's soul and increases your published credits.

This isn't the only section of the Writer's Pyramid, however. As you build your writing career, it's also important to earn income. That's why I recommend adding to your pyramid by spending a portion of your writing efforts each week looking for specific ways to earn income. Target a publisher, study their website, brainstorm three to five brand new ideas that would fit into their product line, and send them a query to ask if they'd like to receive a proposal for any of those ideas. Because you're not actually *writing* a manuscript for this section of the pyramid, however, don't spend as much time at this task as you do each week writing for the no-pay/low-pay markets.

There is one more section of the Writer's Pyramid. It's the smallest section on top. As you're building your writing career, it's important to always be working on your own manuscript for personal fulfillment. This is the one that you're writing just because you want to. This project keeps your writer's heart burning and your energy level high.

If you spend too much time on it each week, however, it will make your pyramid top-heavy and risk the danger of causing your career to crumble to the ground. That's why writing for personal fulfillment occupies the top, smallest section of the Writer's Pyramid. It's on top, too, because it gives you inspiration to keep reaching for the stars. Keep dreaming. Keep daring. Keep writing for personal fulfillment and submitting these manuscripts to the publishers of your dreams. Just be sure you keep this aspect of your writing career in its proper place at the top of the pyramid. Spend the least amount of time on this section each week as you're building your writing career.

This is the model to follow until you land a contract or assignment to write an article or book to earn income. Once you sign a contract, however, the Writer's Pyramid changes.

Writer's Pyramid #2—After a Contract

When you've landed a contract, draw a new triangle on a piece of paper. Once again, draw two horizontal lines across the inside of the triangle so that it is divided into thirds. There is a large section at the base of the triangle, a medium-sized section in the middle, and a small section on top.

- Label the bottom section: Income.

- Label the middle section: No-pay/low-pay markets.

- Label the top section: Personal fulfillment.

Now you'll be spending the majority of your time each week writing for your deadline. This forms the base of your new Writer's Pyramid. You're writing, and you're getting paid for it. That adds up to success for your career.

Just be sure to still attend to your two other goals each week so that you keep getting published frequently and continue to write for personal fulfillment. Allot smaller proportions of time to these two goals, as demonstrated in the pyramid.

When that deadline is finished, if you don't yet have another deadline lined up, refer back to your original triangle (Writer's Pyramid #1). Concentrate most of your time each week on writing for the no-pay/low-pay markets. Also spend a portion of your time targeting new publishers with new queries to try to land your next contract. Be sure to also spend a small amount of time writing for personal fulfillment.

Move back and forth between the two models depending on whether or not you've landed a contract or an assignment to earn income. As you begin to line up contracts and assignments like ducks in a row, you'll use the second model the most. You'll spend the majority of your writing week working on your dead-line to earn income, a smaller amount of time writing to get published, and an even smaller proportion of time writing for personal fulfillment.

Once again, the Writer's Pyramid helps you manage your time and focus your energy on very specific purposes each day in your writing week as you pursue the Triple Crown of Success. Make it your goal to manage your time effectively to keep building the Writer's Pyramid so your career will continue to grow. In the following section, I'll discuss how to learn better time-management skills.

Beginner's Tip

It's okay to work at your own pace to meet each of these three separate goals. Try not to compare yourself with other writers, but explore what pace works best for you. Just be sure to divide your time between the three goals in the recommended proportions if you're trying to build a career.

Professional Track

As your writing skills and editorial contacts increase, you might start writing and getting published frequently in higher-paying periodical markets. These markets, as long as they practically guarantee frequent publication, can replace the lower-paying ones you initially wrote for. However, always try to keep a relationship going with three to five different publishers to get published frequently and regularly. This avoids the syndrome of placing all your eggs in one basket. If an editor leaves or the publisher goes bankrupt, you'll have others to continue with until you find a new one to replace it.

6.2 *Time Management*

You know what priorities and commitments your life holds for you each day. You know your own schedule and what works realistically for you. Whether you're able to write more or less than someone else doesn't determine whether or not you're a writer. You *are* a writer! Even if you haven't yet written anything, you have a writer's heart. Learn effective time management skills by implementing the Writer's Pyramid so that you can find time to write.

The amount of time that you find to write does determine whether you're writing for a hobby or building a career, however. If you're not logging in enough hours each week to build a part-time or full-time career, you are in essence supporting a hobby. That's okay. It's perfectly fine to write as a hobby. But if you want to build a successful writing career, you have to show up at the computer, sit down to type, and write for hours each week.

When my friend found a part-time job, her life suddenly had a new priority. Each week they posted her upcoming schedule on the wall. Each week she had to rearrange her personal life according to her work hours in the week ahead. On some days, we couldn't go out for lunch because she was scheduled to work. On other days, we couldn't take a walk together because she had to go to work. Her work hours came first, and everything else was adjusted to fit around that time frame.

If you want to have a part-time writing career, learn to treat your schedule as my friend had to treat her new job. Post a weekly calendar. Schedule in your hours of writing for the week ahead. If you want to have a full-time writing career, schedule in 40 hours of writing each week.

Perhaps you already have a full-time job and want to transition into building a writing career. It's best if you think of this transition as a time when you'll be working two jobs instead of just one.

I've known so many writers who either don't work at all or who already work at another job. They want to establish a career as a writer. They spend time working on their own manuscripts whenever they have a free moment. However, most aren't willing to schedule in blocks of writing time each week into their already over-packed calendar. They hope they'll just sort of magically break into the world of publishing and suddenly start earning the big bucks.

It doesn't work like that.

Writing as a career is just like any other career. You have to show up for work certain hours each week if you want to get paid. If you want to build a successful writing career, you have to manage your time just as if you got hired to work at a local business. Yes, you call the shots and determine which hours work best for you each week. But you have to show up at the computer and write each week or you're essentially writing as a hobby. Once again, that's fine. It's okay to write as a hobby. But if you want to build a successful writing career, you have to make it a priority to schedule in hours each week to write.

Unlike my friend who had no choice over which hours her employer scheduled her to work in the week ahead, you are in charge of scheduling your own hours. If you're a self-motivated person, no problem. If you're not a self-motivated person, it's not a bad thing, necessarily. It's just that you'll have to work extra-hard to make sure you schedule in your upcoming commitment to write each week and actually show up at the computer to type.

The most basic way I've found to best manage my time as I'm building my Writer's Pyramid is to use a calendar. Most jobs operate by their employee calendar, and the job of writing benefits from using a calendar, as well. Sometimes I purchase a special, themed calendar that I use for my daily, weekly, and monthly schedule. Other times, I print out colorful calendars on my computer's publishing program. I add clipart and inspirational quotes pertaining to my current writing projects. Whichever calendar you use, find one that suits your lifestyle and personal interests.

With calendar in hand, schedule in the hours you will write for the week ahead. If you want to build a part-time writing career, I suggest scheduling in at least five hours minimum each week. If you want to build a full-time writing career, block out 40 hours for writing in the week ahead.

Now that you have your writing hours scheduled for the week ahead, it's time to implement the Writer's Pyramid and determine your focus. By having a specific focus for the time you plan to sit down and write, you can jumpstart your career with success. In the next section, I'll show you how.

Beginner's Tip

Learn to maximize even the smallest segments of available time. Schedule in 15-minute periods of writing while you're waiting to pick up your kids from school or are on your lunch break at work.

Professional Track

If you have numerous writing-related commitments already scheduled on your calendar such as book signings, school visits, or writer's workshops, be sure to make it a priority to schedule on your calendar actual time to write, as well. Unless you're actually writing on a continuous and regular basis, your career could be in danger of drying up.

6.3 Focus

Now that you have your writing schedule for the week ahead, it's time to assign a specific task to focus on each hour you'll be writing. Once again, the Writer's Pyramid works hand-in-hand with the Triple Crown of Success (using three separate strategies to meet three separate goals). In essence, the Writer's Pyramid helps you manage your time and focus your energies on very specific purposes each day in your writing week as you pursue the Triple Crown of Success. Implementing these strategies, you can follow your dreams and build a successful writing career.

Whether you're scheduled to write five hours next week or five eight-hour days, learn to divide your schedule into proportions that will guarantee success. Using the Writer's Pyramid as your guide, remember that if you do not yet have a deadline to earn income for a contract or assignment, use Writer's Pyramid #1. Draw the triangle, or pyramid, so that it's divided into thirds. Label the bottom section *No-pay/low-pay markets*, the middle section *Income*, and the top section *Personal fulfillment*.

If you're scheduled to write five hours next week, plan to focus three hours writing for the no-pay/low-pay markets. Look on your calendar and write this assignment down for your first three hours of writing.

Using this same schedule, plan to focus one hour writing for income. Look on your calendar and write this assignment down for your next hour of writing.

Finally, plan to focus one hour writing for personal fulfillment. Look on your calendar and write this assignment down for your last hour of writing.

If you're planning on writing full time and have scheduled in 40 hours for writing next week, divide your calendar into similar proportions, using Writer's Pyramid #1 as your guide. Plan to focus three eight-hour days writing for the no-pay/low-pay markets. Write this assignment down on your calendar for your first three days of writing.

Using this same schedule, plan to focus one day writing for income. Write this assignment down on the calendar for your next day of writing.

Finally, plan to focus one day writing for personal fulfillment. Write this assignment down on the calendar for your last day of writing.

Of course, you may have scheduled a different amount of hours on your calendar to write for the week ahead. Using the Writer's Pyramid as a guide, divide your schedule into proportions so that you're writing mostly to get published, spending some time targeting publishers to hopefully land a contract and earn income, and writing for personal fulfillment.

If you land a contract to earn income in the days ahead, be sure to change your model to Writer's Pyramid #2 (bottom section *Income*, middle section *No-pay/low-pay markets*, top section *Personal fulfillment*), so that you're now spending most of your time writing for your deadline each week. Spend a smaller portion of time writing for no-pay/low-pay markets and for personal fulfillment.

Follow this schedule and this focus for your writing each week. Be sure to post your new calendar for each new upcoming week with segments of time blocked out for you to sit down and write. In the next section I'll explain in more detail how you can use these building blocks effectively to help you accomplish your purpose of building a successful career as a children's writer.

Beginner's Tip

Each time you write for longer periods of time than you originally planned each week, give yourself a small reward for a job well done.

Professional Track

Perhaps you've had success as a writer but not yet achieved the level of published credits or income you want to have as a writer. It could be a tough decision, but you might need to step down from other non-writing related commitments to give you more time to write.

6.4 A Schedule with Purpose

You're using a calendar and are learning how to manage your time as a writer. You've got the Writer's Pyramid to help you focus your energy on separate goals in proportions that will maximize your success. Now I'll show you in a more detailed manner how to implement the Triple Crown of Success into your writing schedule with purpose so that you can build the foundation for a solid and successful writing career in just one month.

Three-Week Cycle

If you work full-time and want to make the transition to a writing career, but can't schedule large chunks of time each day to write, there are other options. One is to adapt the strategies I suggest in this chapter to work on a three-week cycle, just one hour each day.

For Week One, schedule one hour for writing each day on your calendar, Monday through Friday. In Week One, you will still be building the foundation of getting published on a frequent basis.

For Week Two, schedule one hour for writing each day on your calendar, Monday through Friday. Spend your time targeting a publisher and submitting a query to land a potential contract that pays. You'll build the foundation of writing to earn income.

For Week Three, you'll build the foundation of writing just for fun. Schedule in one hour each day, Monday through Friday, and write just for the fun of it.

For Week Four, start the cycle over again. By writing with purpose and with a plan for your one hour each day, working toward three separate goals each different week, you will be able to lay the foundation for a solid writing career. You'll be writing for the Triple Crown of Success. Plus, it will suit your busy schedule and hopefully not be overwhelming.

In Just One Month

You can lay a solid foundation to build a successful writing career in just one month! This new schedule will work best if you are able to carve out at least 15 hours each week to write. If that's an impossible task at this point in your schedule, don't despair! Continue to build your Writer's Pyramid and write with focus each week for the hours that you can commit to. When you're ready to increase your writing workload to at least 15 hours each week, come back to this section for a practical, step-by-step guide on how to write with purpose.

If, however, you're already committed to writing full-time, you're ready to go. Hop on board and join the fun. Write with purpose each week, and build the foundation for a solid and successful writing career in just one month.

First, print out or purchase a calendar of the next four weeks. Have this be your writing calendar. Post your writing schedule for Week One by blocking out one hour for writing each day, Monday through Friday. (Of course, if you have more time allotted in your schedule for writing, please feel free to spend longer each day accomplishing each task.)

Week One

On Monday, spend your hour researching no-pay/low-pay periodical markets. Pick one periodical to target.

On Tuesday, spend your hour reading your target periodical. Pick one kind of article you'd like to try to write for it, whether it be the recipe corner, the crafts page, or a devotional. Type out a sample, word-for-word, of an article similar to the one you want to write. This exercise helps train your brain to write for this specific target publisher.

On Wednesday, spend half of your hour brainstorming ideas to write for your target periodical. Then spend the next half hour organizing your ideas into an outline for the article you want to write.

On Thursday, spend your hour writing the first draft of your article or preparing a query.

On Friday, spend your hour editing, revising, and completing the final draft of your manuscript or query. Submit the query, or write a short cover letter and submit it with your manuscript to your target publisher.

It's amazing what you can accomplish writing just one hour each day in one week!

Week Two

For Week Two, on your writing calendar, block out two hours for writing each day, Monday through

Friday. In Week One, you built the foundation of getting published on a regular basis. In Week Two, you'll build the foundation of landing contracts for deadlines to write books and magazine articles that pay.

Remember why it's important to land contracts before you write the manuscript? Because in the real world of career writing, that's how writers earn their pay. They land a contract by pitching an idea. They discuss the details and tweak the idea to suit the editor's needs. Then, they write the manuscript. Talk with most career writers and that's what they'll tell you about how it actually works in order to earn a steady and substantial income.

For Week Two, you will continue writing one hour each day to build on your foundation of getting published on a frequent basis. You will also add one hour each day to build your foundation of landing contracts for deadlines. Here's what to do.

On Monday, spend one hour writing for a no-pay/low-pay periodical. Spend it researching no-pay/low-pay periodical markets. Pick one periodical to target.

Spend your second hour writing to land a contract. Spend it researching the market. Read market guides and writer's magazines until you find a publisher who accepts queries that you'd like to write for. Pick one publisher to target.

On Tuesday, spend one hour writing for a no-pay/low-pay periodical. Spend it reading your target periodical. Pick one kind of article you'd like to try to write for it, whether it be the recipe corner, the crafts page, or the devotional. Type out a sample of the type of article you want to write. This exercise helps train your brain to write for this specific target publisher.

Spend the second hour writing to land a contract. Spend it reading your target publisher's product line. Use the "search inside the book" feature on Amazon.com. Get your publisher's books from your local library. After you've spent time reading, type out samples from the format you'd like to pattern your upcoming manuscript after. Again, this exercise helps train your brain to write for this specific target publisher.

On Wednesday, spend one hour writing for a no-pay/low-pay periodical. Spend half an hour brainstorming ideas to write for your target periodical. Then spend the next half hour organizing your ideas into an outline for the article you want to write.

Spend the second hour writing to land a contract. Spend it brainstorming a manuscript idea that fits like a glove into your target publisher's product line. To help you get ideas, browse through their website. Make a list of titles they've already done and try to think of titles that will fit into that list that they haven't yet done. Choose three to five potential ideas that might fit into their product line.

On Thursday, spend one hour writing for a no-pay/low-pay periodical. Spend it writing the first draft of your article or query.

Spend the second hour writing to land a contract. Spend it writing a paragraph about each of your three to five ideas to flesh them out.

On Friday, spend one hour writing for a no-pay/low-pay periodical. Spend it editing and revising your manuscript or query. Submit the query, or write a short cover letter and submit it with your manuscript to your target publisher.

Spend the second hour writing to land a contract. Spend it writing a query to send to your target publisher. In the query, state that you've been browsing their website, studying their product line, and reading their books. Explain that you have three to five ideas that might fit into their product line. Include the paragraph you wrote for each of your ideas. Ask the editor if she would be interested in receiving a proposal for one of those ideas. Check the target publisher's writer's guidelines to see if they take e-mail queries. If they do, e-mail your query. If not, snail mail it.

Whew! What a lot you have accomplished in just two short weeks. You are well on your way to building the foundation for a solid writing career.

Week Three

For Week Three, on your writing calendar, block out three hours for writing each day, Monday through Friday. In Week One, you built the foundation of getting published on a regular basis. In Week Two, you built the foundation of landing contracts for deadlines to write books and magazine articles that pay. In Week Three, you'll build the foundation of writing just for fun. It's always important, as a writer, to write for fun. That's why you got started writing in the first place, right? If you leave that out of your writing career, you'll be in danger of quitting writing altogether.

For Week Three, you will continue writing one hour each day to build on your foundation of getting published on a frequent basis. You will continue writing one hour each day to build your foundation of landing contracts for deadlines. You will also write one hour each day just for fun. Here's what to do.

Follow the same schedule as the previous week for your first two hours each day. Spend your third hour writing just for fun. Go ahead! Write anything you like. Research for that historical novel you've always wanted to write. Type out that poem that's running around in your head. Write that inspirational devotion you want to share. Just write for the sheer joy of it.

By Saturday, you'll be amazed at all you have accomplished. Just think of it—three weeks ago you might have been in the doldrums because you never seemed to have anything to show for yourself as a writer. Now in just three weeks, you're writing with focus, purpose, and fun. You're experiencing what it means to write for the Triple Crown of Success. You're well on your way to building the foundation for a solid writing career.

Week Four

Now it's time to adjust everything you've learned the last three weeks into the model of the Writer's Pyramid.

Once again, schedule your hours for writing a week ahead on your calendar. Block off three hours to write each day, Monday through Friday, so you're writing at least 15 hours this week.

Refer to your Writer's Pyramid. If you haven't yet landed a contract or assignment to earn income, use Writer's Pyramid #1. Spend Monday, Tuesday, and Wednesday writing for the no-pay/low-pay markets. Spend Thursday researching a target publisher and submitting a query in hopes of landing a potential contract. On Friday, write for personal fulfillment.

Of course, when you start landing contracts, you'll have to change to Writer's Pyramid #2, so you're spending more time writing to earn an income. But by then, you'll be used to writing three hours every day, so you'll be able to meet those deadlines.

Beginner's Tip

Sometimes life gets out of control and you simply can't find time to write. Even one hour a day seems daunting. At times like these, instead of banging my head against the wall, I simplify my goals. I make it my goal to write 15 minutes each day, Monday through Friday. That's all. Those 15 minutes a day make a huge difference, however. It keeps me progressing forward on my three main goals. It keeps me in touch with my writing project. It keeps me connected with my writing until I can get through that season of chaos and back on track to writing three hours a day.

Professional Track

After you've landed that contract and are writing for a deadline, don't wait until your current manuscript is finished before you start looking for another project to earn income. As your deadline draws close, start the target publisher/send query cycle again until you land the next contract.

Chapter 7
Short-term Goals

7.1 Motivation

Are you a brand new wannabe writer? Or have you felt the itch to write for years and years? Whichever age and stage you're at today, you can get motivated to set realistic goals and meet them successfully. You can catch the vision, fire up your enthusiasm, and pursue those dreams that tug at your heartstrings. You can build a successful career as a children's writer!

Meeting goals successfully is all about motivation. What motivates you? Are you a self-motivator? That's a big plus in this profession. Or do you while away the hours you're alone tending to trivial tasks instead of actually showing up at the computer to type new material each day? If so, don't despair! You can discover ways to get motivated to chase after your dreams.

Writing is a lonely and solitary occupation. There just isn't any way around it—this job demands countless hours spent alone with yourself for days on end. Throughout history, numerous writers experienced depression. It's not any different today.

The good news is that there are many creative ways to add motivation into your day so that you're inspired and encouraged to move forward to meet your goals.

Rewards are one of the most basic forms of motivation. Are you rewarding yourself for each small step you accomplish as a writer? If not, then start today. Do you like to garden? Set a goal for yourself today such as writing for one hour focused on your strategy to earn income. If you meet your goal, reward yourself with an hour in your garden. Are you involved in a historical fiction listserve? Set a goal for today to write the first draft of the article for your no-pay/low-pay market. If you meet your goal, reward yourself by reading the e-mails on your historical fiction listserve. Do you like to walk? Set a goal for today to work on that manuscript for personal fulfillment. If you meet your goal, reward yourself by taking a walk with a friend.

Daily rewards are great. They help you meet daily writing goals. Weekly rewards are good, too. This past year I decided to decorate my kitchen with chickens. So each week that I met my weekly goals, I rewarded myself with a shopping trip to purchase one small decoration with a chicken motif for my kitchen. It really got me motivated during a dry and dismal writing slump. A weekly reward doesn't have to cost a penny, though. You can reward yourself with reading your favorite book after you've met your writing goals for the week.

Long-term rewards can be very motivating as well. I don't enjoy housework. Yet I work out of my own home. Over the years, writer friends and writer groups have met in my house. So I set up a long-term reward for myself. When I reached a certain income level, I hired a housecleaner. Not only does it motivate me to maintain that income level, but it frees me and gives me more hours to write. I can also use it as a tax deduction. It's a win-win reward!

A scrapbook can be very motivating. Two years ago, I started making a scrapbook just of my writing. From positive notes by editors to photos of my writers' groups to exciting news about contracts and publication of new books, making a scrapbook added a wonderful dimension of motivation to my writing life. An extra bonus is that if I'm feeling discouraged, I pull it out and get encouraged all over again. Then I'm energized to get back to my goals.

A goal notebook helps motivate, as well. A local writer friend encouraged everyone in our critique group to create one. Maintaining a list of your goals promotes a positive focus on where you want to go as a writer. Journaling the process keeps you in touch with your writer's soul. Tracking accomplishments helps you enjoy the journey and treasure each moment of achievement.

Accountability with a critique group can be very motivating. Sharing your goals with others who will encourage you and check in with you helps you stay on track.

Creating an inspirational environment can also be very motivating. Candles, music, posters, encouraging quotes, or a mascot for your current project can all add up to surround you with motivation to sit down and write.

If you're not a self-motivated person, you can still find ways to bring out your best attempts for meeting those goals. Partner with a co-author. This provides one-on-one accountability and brings a motivational coach on board your project.

Land a deadline, even for the no-pay/low-pay markets. There's nothing like a looming calendar date to motivate you to write.

Explore *why* you lack motivation to meet your writing goals. Then try to discover something that *will* motivate you and meet that need. For instance, if you lack motivation to write because you feel too lonely in your house when the kids are gone at school, conquer the loneliness. Grab your laptop, go to your local coffee shop, and write there each day instead.

So come on! Let's get motivated! Let's set up realistic goals to accomplish important achievements and make our writers' dreams a reality. In the next section, I'll help you get started.

Beginner's Tip

Make a list of small, free rewards that you can use to motivate yourself to meet daily goals. Choose one item from your list each day as a reward for a job well done.

Professional Track

If you're already earning big bucks as a writer but currently lack motivation, take a careful look at your finances. Are you using all your money to help pay the bills? Budget a practical way that you can use a portion of your writing income to save up and purchase something meaningful. This could add just the motivational spark you need.

7.2 Daily and Weekly Goals

Setting small, short-term goals for yourself as a writer is extremely beneficial. How do you "eat an elephant"? One bite at a time. How do you write a book? One word at a time. You can accomplish great achievements as a children's writer. You can build a successful career. One word and one day and one week at a time.

Implementing the models to pursue the Triple Crown of Success and to build the Writer's Pyramid will help you lay a firm foundation. Learn to use three separate strategies to meet three separate goals. Balance the time you spend on each by scheduling your week ahead and assigning a specific purpose to each hour of writing.

Each weekend, I like to sit down with my goal notebook and my calendar. I review my short-term goals as well as my monthly and yearly goals. I block in my hours for writing on my calendar for the week ahead and jot down the goals I hope to meet during that time.

Each evening during the week, I once again sit down with my goal notebook and my calendar. I think about the scheduled times I'll be writing the next day. I assign specific tasks to each hour I plan to write. I refer to the Triple Crown of Success and the Writer's Pyramid constantly to keep track of how much time I'm spending meeting each separate goal. This helps me focus and gives me purpose as I write.

Sometimes when I attempt to meet a certain daily goal, it takes longer than I anticipated. For instance, an article that I thought would take me one full day of writing actually takes three. I adjust my daily goals to meet these unexpected developments.

Other times, something happens to interrupt the time I had planned to write. Our dog wakes up sick and I have to take her to the vet. Once again, I adjust my daily goals to accommodate life's unexpected interruptions. Because I sit down each evening and plan for the day ahead, I can make quick and effective adjustments in my daily goals so that I can hopefully achieve my weekly goal.

Most of all, I try to keep my daily and weekly goals within my reach. I want to accomplish my goals. If I find myself consistently not meeting my goals, I trim them so I *can* meet them. I'd rather adjust my daily and weekly goals and frequently accomplish tasks in small chunks than set goals so high that I'm stretched too thin and am in danger of giving up altogether because I feel overwhelmed.

Take for instance, the time the dog was sick and I had to go to the vet instead of meeting my writing goal for the day. Let's say my weekly goal included submitting one manuscript to a no-pay/low-pay publisher, sending a query to a book publisher to attempt to land a contract for income, and writing one chapter for my manuscript for personal fulfillment. If my daily goal had been to spend all day choosing a new target publisher, studying their website, exploring their products, brainstorming three to five ideas that would fit into their product line, and submitting a query to the editor, I wouldn't have accomplished my goal because I had to go to the vet.

If the next day's goal was to research and then write a new chapter in the middle grade novel I'm working on for personal fulfillment, I would readjust that day's goal so I could accomplish my weekly goal. I would limit my time studying the target publisher's website and try to come up with one to three very simple ideas and submit my query. Then, instead of spending several hours on research for my middle grade novel, I would limit it to one hour and spend the remaining time writing that chapter. I could fact-check during later editing to make up the difference. I trimmed down two day's worth of goals into one day so I could accomplish both in the time that I had.

As I mentioned, I always keep in mind my monthly and yearly goals as I'm determining my daily and weekly goals. Read the next section to learn more about setting productive monthly and yearly goals to help build a successful career.

Beginner's Tip

A great daily goal to set if you want to write a novel or full-length book is to write one page every day, Monday through Friday. By the end of the year, you'll have over 250 pages.

Professional Track

If you already get published frequently but want to earn more income through writing, readjust your Writer's Pyramid. Spend most of your time trying to land your next contract. Set a daily goal to send a query to one different target publisher each day. Start each morning by choosing your next publisher to target. Study their website. Brainstorm three to five ideas that would fit into their product line. By the end of the day, type these up into a query and submit it to their editor. Target a different publisher each day until an editor responds and asks to see a proposal for one of your ideas. As soon as that proposal is out the door, continue this cycle for your daily goals until you land a contract.

7.3 Monthly and Yearly Goals

Whether you write for a minimum number of five hours each week or write full time for a 40-hour week, you can set monthly and yearly goals in place to build a successful writing career. Establishing these goals and reaching to accomplish them will help you feel like you're in control of your career as a writer. In an industry that often feels overwhelming and out-of-control, this is a huge benefit.

Let's start by looking at the year ahead. What do you hope to accomplish in the next twelve months as a writer? Refer to the Triple Crown of Success and the Writer's Pyramid as a guide. Remember the three reasons every writer writes: to get published, to earn income, and for personal fulfillment. Utilize a separate strategy to meet each of your goals on a daily basis as I have discussed. Then determine your yearly goals for each and break this down into monthly goals.

Goals for the Beginning or Five-Hour-a-Week Writer

If you are a beginning writer or only have five hours a week at most to write, here are realistic suggestions for setting yearly and monthly goals:

- **Goal: Write for Personal Fulfillment**
  Make it your goal to complete a designated portion of your own, personal manuscript by the end of the year. Break this pre-determined amount into twelve equal chunks that you can accomplish each month.

- **Goal: Write to Get Published**
  Make it your year-long goal to look for three to five no-pay/low-pay markets and get published one to three times in each. Break this down into a monthly goal of writing and submitting one or two manuscripts for this market each month.

- **Goal: Write to Earn Income**
  Try to land one book contract or high-paying periodical assignment in the year ahead. Break this down into a monthly goal of sending a query to one different target publisher each month with a list of three to five ideas that would fit well into their product line. If an editor responds and wants to see a proposal for one of your ideas, prepare the proposal, submit it, and then return to your cycle of sending out one new query to a different target publisher each month. Continue this cycle until you actually land a contract or assignment.

Goals for the Full-time Writer

If you plan to write full-time for a 40-hour workweek in the year ahead, here are realistic suggestions for setting yearly and monthly goals:

- **Goal: Write for Personal Fulfillment**
  Make it your goal to complete a designated portion of your own, personal manuscript by the end of the year. Break this pre-determined amount into twelve equal chunks that you can accomplish each month.

- **Goal: Write to Get Published**
  Make it your year-long goal to write for three to five no-pay/low-pay markets and get published

frequently. Break this down into a monthly goal of writing and submitting three to five manuscripts for this market each month.

- **Goal: Write to Earn Income**
  Try to land book contracts or high-paying periodical assignments throughout the year ahead so that you are earning a designated income. Break this down into a monthly goal of sending a query to one different target publisher each week within the upcoming month.

Sometimes I reinstate a cycle of sending out queries to target publishers toward the end of a current contract.

Other times, I like to spend the first few months of the year contacting potential target publishers nearly daily until I have my deadlines lined up like ducks in a row. I contact work-for-hire publishers for quick cash and also royalty publishers to build up a potential income base for the years ahead.

Sometimes I submit queries to publishers I've already worked with. Other times I branch out to send queries to brand new publishers. Sometimes I include agents in my cycle of submissions.

I keep making my contacts and submitting my queries until I have deadlines spaced out on my calendar for the upcoming year.

Beginner's Tip

If you receive rejections for your submissions to the no-pay/low-pay markets, or get a rejection for a proposal an editor requested, just move on and try different publishers. Rejections to a writer are like weeds to a gardener. If you plant a garden, weeds will grow. If you send in submissions, rejections will accumulate. Cheer up! A rejection is proof that you're a real, actual factual, honest-to-goodness writer.

Professional Track

If you're already getting published frequently and know you'll earn enough income for the year ahead from projected royalties, this might be a great opportunity to spend more time writing that manuscript you've always wanted to write. Go ahead! Write the book of your dreams in the year ahead. It might even be fun to self-publish it when it's done. Take advantage of this time and write mainly for the goal of personal fulfillment. Be sure to keep your foot in the door with your other publishers, however, so you can get back on track with them at the end of the year.

Chapter 8
Target Periodicals

8.1 The Periodical Market

Writing for the periodical market can provide a steady source of income for regular feature authors. It's also a great market for the goal of getting published as well as writing for personal fulfillment. There are a variety of children's magazines to choose from filled with exciting opportunities for writers. If you'd like to target periodical publishers, there are practical steps you can take to help make your efforts a success.

Get Organized

First of all, get organized. You're going to take lots of notes and gather a variety of materials on your journey, so you want to keep it organized as you go. I like to use pocket file folders when I'm preparing to target a new periodical publisher. The five-inch expandable version is large enough to hold samples of my target magazine, too. Inside the pocket folder, place several file folders to hold important information you'll find on your search. Label each one as you fill it for easy reference. Start with a file folder for Potential Publishers and one for Ideas.

Research the Periodical Market

You can begin your research of the periodical market by studying the *Children's Writer's & Illustrator's Market* or *Magazine Markets for Children's Writers*. Don't limit your search to the market guides, however. There are numerous periodicals in a variety of markets such as major newspapers, web magazines, and curriculum-related material. Many have columns or entire publications geared for a children's audience. Explore a variety of avenues in your search.

Make a Chart

Make a chart to compile a list of potential publishers that interest you. Start out by creating a blank Excel spreadsheet or draw a chart by hand. Make columns for: Periodical, Editor, E-mail, Website, Queries, Circulation, Target Age, Features, Terms, Payment, and Miscellaneous Notes.

Try to fit your chart on one page using landscape view or horizontal orientation for the page layout. Use abbreviations or small font to fit the title at the top of each column. Make your rows with enough height for you to write in. Place eight to ten rows on one page. Add borders for all the columns and rows, and print out your easy-to-use chart. Photocopy several blank charts and store these in a file folder to use as you need them.

Sit down with your market guide in a comfortable chair. Read through the list of periodicals, jotting down key information on your chart as you go.

- Write the periodical's name under the Periodical column.

- Write the acquisition editor's name under the Editor column.

- If one is provided, write down that editor's e-mail under the E-mail column.

- Write the URL of its website under the Website column.

- Under the Queries column, mark whether or not they accept unsolicited queries.

- Write the number of subscriptions it has under Circulation.

- Under Target Age, write down what ages the periodical targets.

- Under the Feature column, write down notes about various features the periodical has such as Fiction, Nonfiction, Puzzles, or Crafts.

- Write down which rights they purchase under Terms.

- Write down their payment range under Payment.

- Add anything else of interest under Miscellaneous Notes.

Because you're using a small chart for all this information, don't go into lengthy detail. Just jot down enough of a note in each column to jog your memory about each publisher on your list. Not every publisher will list every detail in your market guide. Leave those spaces blank for now.

Now that you've spent time researching the periodical market, it's time to choose one publisher to target. Find out how to do this in the next section.

Beginner's Tip

Remember the Triple Crown of Success. If you're researching publishers to get published, make a list of no-pay/low-pay periodicals. If you're researching publishers for income, list any periodical that accepts queries, offers a substantial income, and where you think, "I can try to write an article for them!" If you're researching publishers to write for personal fulfillment, list whichever periodical catches your eye.

Professional Track

Network with members of your critique group to research periodicals as potential target publishers. Share and compare your results. It can be a lot more fun to target a publisher together with other members of your group.

8.2 Choose Your Target Publisher

After you have a number of potential publishers listed on your chart, choose one as your potential target publisher. Treasure the moment of discovery when you determine which periodical to target. You're making important progress toward building a successful writing career.

Be sure that if you're targeting a periodical publisher to earn income, they are open to receiving unsolicited query letters.

If your target publisher pays the big bucks but requires a completed manuscript submission, target them for personal fulfillment at first. Then, if they accept your manuscript, you can try to establish a relationship with the editor and start pitching ideas to land contracts or assignments so you're getting paid while you write. That's the strategy to use with the Triple Crown of Success for earning income as you build your writing career.

Get Issues of the Periodical

Once you choose your target publisher, it's time to get current issues of their periodical. If you don't yet have three to five current samples, call the publisher to order several. A year's back issues are ideal, but not always easily attainable. Be sure to mention you're a freelance author, and they might send you sample issues for free. You can also find certain magazines at your library's used bookstore, at the local magazine rack, or for sale online. Store these sample issues in your pocket file folder.

Visit the Magazine's Website

Visit the magazine's website if they have one. Print out their submissions guidelines or writer's guidelines. Sometimes these guidelines are hard to find on a magazine website because the website is designed to appeal to their customer, not a writer. Dig around under such links as "About us" or "Contact us" until you find the information you need. Many magazines center around a certain theme each issue. Be sure to print out their theme list if they operate this way.

Look for their author's terms, too. How much do they pay for their various features? Do they purchase all rights, first rights, reprint rights, or...? All rights means that they completely own the copyright to your article and can use it however they wish. First rights (also known by such names as First North

American Rights or First World Rights) means that you keep the copyright for your article but give the publisher permission to publish it first. Reprint rights means that the article has been published elsewhere already, and you're giving permission for this periodical to publish it once more.

Update Your Chart

Print out all pertinent information and store it in your file folders. If the website lists different information than what you previously wrote on your chart, change your chart to match the website. A website is usually more current than a market guide and can reflect important recent editorial changes that took place after the market guide went to print.

Read Your Target Periodical

Take time to read your target periodical samples. After you enjoy an initial read, go back and study the various issues with your imaginary magnifying glass in hand. First stop should be the carefully hidden list of editors, subscription information, and copyright information. This is called the masthead and is often in very small print. Compare this list of editors to the names of the writers who wrote the articles throughout the magazine. If these same editors are the ones who wrote various articles, the publisher might not be open to receiving unsolicited articles for those particular features. Those features might be written in-house. Try to find features that appear to be written by a variety of authors. Choose one that interests you to write. Type out this article or feature, word-for-word. This exercise helps train your brain to write with the same voice and format that the publisher already likes.

Now that you've chosen your target periodical publisher and examined samples of current issues, you're ready to come up with a list of fresh, new ideas that could fit into their magazine. Read the next section for tips on brainstorming.

Beginner's Tip

I often type out similar articles to the one I hope to write, and reread the same ones again and again as I'm working on targeting a specific publisher. It helps me focus on what a publisher already likes and guides me as I take careful aim.

Professional Track

Build a stash of sample current issues of potential magazines you want to target. Keep an eye out for bargain deals at local thrift stores or in libraries' used bookstores.

8.3 Brainstorm Ideas

Now it's time to brainstorm for your own ideas. Even if you've had difficulty inventing new ideas in the past, the following tips will help you experience success now. By tracking topics a periodical has already published in past issues, you can more easily think of potential ideas that could fit into future issues so you can catch an editor's eye.

As you're searching for ideas, it's important *not* to include manuscripts you've already written. The goal of targeting a publisher is to brainstorm ideas that an editor wants, not try to sell them manuscripts you already wrote. Sure, if you start getting published with this publisher and establish a relationship with this editor, *then* you can tell them about a manuscript you already wrote that you think would be a good fit for them. But targeting a publisher isn't about finding one to submit your manuscript to. *Targeting a publisher is all about finding out what a publisher already publishes and coming up with ideas to fit into that editor's current needs and interests.*

The Wagon Wheel

On a blank sheet of paper, draw a small circle with a dozen spokes coming out of it such as the spokes inside of a pioneer wagon wheel.

In the center of the small circle, write the name of the type of feature you just typed out and that you'd be interested in writing such as a puzzle, recipe, fiction story, nonfiction article, interview, mystery, etc.

Along the right hand side of the paper, make a list of topics that have already been covered in the magazine samples you've read. For instance, if your target periodical has a nonfiction article each issue, make a list of the topics you've seen for the nonfiction articles in their current issues such as: how candy is made, the history of toothpaste, and the history of paper.

Then, on the spokes of your wagon wheel, write down potential ideas for nonfiction articles you could pitch to the editor that could complement the topics they've already published. Your list might include such potential new topics as: where Christmas trees come from, the history of the stapler, and how a modern-day dairy operates.

If you find yourself staring into space, unable to come up with fresh, new ideas, try taking a visit to a local bookstore, visiting your library, or browsing an online bookstore. Explore similar topics for your magazine's target age until you find potential ones to write on the spokes of your wagon wheel. Choose three to five of these ideas that interest you the most.

Contact the Publisher with Your Ideas

If you're targeting a periodical for income, you have the option of simply sending the publisher a list of your ideas to choose from. Or, you can flesh out those three to five ideas by writing out a short paragraph about each one. Write each paragraph specifically targeted to your publisher so that the editor can get a quick grasp of how your idea could fit into her magazine.

In the next section, I'll show you how to contact the publisher about your new ideas. You're ready to either send in a query or write your manuscript and submit it.

Beginner's Tip

If ideas don't come easily to you, create a file box of ideas. Stock your file box with blank index cards. On each index card, write down one idea. Start by creating cards for general topics that interest you such as soccer, gardening, bird watching, quilting, or golfing. Add specific ideas over the days ahead as they come to you.

During the brainstorming process, dig through your idea file box. Pull out an idea card such as "soccer." Ask yourself, "Could I write an article about soccer that might fit into this periodical's feature?" If it's a recipe corner, you could write a recipe that soccer moms could serve during a party after the game. If it's a puzzle, it could be a word search for soccer terms. If it's a biography feature, it could be a biography of a famous soccer star.

Use your idea file to help jumpstart ideas for whatever periodical you're targeting.

> ## *Professional Track*

If you've had success getting published on a certain topic before, brainstorm ways you could use previous research to write a brand new article for your target periodical.

8.4 Contact the Publisher

Writers at all stages of their career feel apprehensive or scared at the thought of contacting a publisher. It helps to picture an editor sitting at her desk wishing someone would just send her something that she's looking for. Many editors receive countless manuscripts that writers submit blindly without even considering the focus and format the publisher prefers.

Since you have spent time targeting your publisher, however, you have the advantage. Your query or manuscript submission can stand head and shoulders above the rest of the slush pile, or stack of unsolicited manuscripts, because you have been doing your homework. Good for you!

Remember the Triple Crown of Success

Remember the Triple Crown of Success: Use three separate strategies to meet three separate goals. If you're targeting this publisher for personal fulfillment or for a no-pay/low-pay market to get published, you have the option of first sending in a query or submitting the completed manuscript. You might want to try your hand at writing and submitting a completed manuscript first. Go for it! As a guide, use the sample features in the magazine similar to the one you want to write.

If you're targeting this publisher for income, write a query letter to send to your target publisher. In the query, state that you've been studying their magazines. Mention your published credits if you have any. Explain that you have three to five ideas that might fit into their publication. You have the option of simply sending the publisher a list of your ideas to choose from. Or, you can flesh out those three to five ideas by writing out a short paragraph about each one. Write each paragraph specifically targeted to your publisher so that the editor can get a quick grasp of how your idea could fit into her magazine.

Ask the editor if she would be interested in receiving a manuscript submission on any of those ideas. If the publisher accepts e-mail queries, always e-mail yours. It's free and it often receives a faster response. If not, send it via postal mail with a self-addressed, stamped envelope, or SASE, inside.

After you have submitted your query, be sure to continue building your Writer's Pyramid so you can build a successful writing career. Spend time working each week pursuing all three goals. Write new material each week for the no-pay/low-pay market to build published credits. If you're not yet writing under a contract, spend time each week submitting a steady stream of queries to target publishers with specific ideas to fit into their unique product line until you land a contract to get paid while you write. And always devote a portion of time each week writing new material for a project for personal fulfillment.

When the Editor Replies

If the editor replies to your query and requests either a more formal proposal or a completed manuscript, answer right away via the same method she contacted you and thank her for her response. Tell her an estimated arrival date of your proposal or manuscript. Don't be afraid to use this opportunity to ask her a question or two that you might have about the next step.

Proposals and Manuscripts

A typical proposal for a periodical includes a more detailed synopsis of your idea than what was presented in your query. For nonfiction proposals, an outline is often preferred. State how your manuscript will fit into the target publication. Include a small sample of your writing such as a short section of the proposed article.

If the editor asks you to submit a completed manuscript for her review without offering you a contract, consider the time and effort it will take you to write this manuscript.

If it would require traveling or other up-front expenses to complete it, communicate with the editor and ask either for a contract to write the manuscript or a kill fee that they agree to pay you even if they reject it in the end.

If your manuscript doesn't require an extraordinary amount of time or expense to write, the editor probably is asking you to submit a completed manuscript on spec, unless she offers you a contract in her reply. On spec means it's on speculation. She still might reject your submission even though she requested it. Many magazines operate by assigning on spec articles. The benefit of submitting a submission on spec, however, is that the editor has a vested interest in your manuscript by this point and will probably be willing to work with you to revise it to better suit her purposes if it originally falls short.

Because each periodical is unique, often with one-of-a-kind features suited specifically to its focus, the best way to learn how to write the actual manuscript for your target publisher is to use their own articles as a guide. Dissect the current published articles similar to the one you plan to write. Read them over and over again. Follow the format of that specific feature closely. If five experts are quoted in that feature, then quote five experts in yours. If that feature has two sidebars, include two sidebars with yours. Use samples of your periodical to help you hit your target in the bull's-eye.

To help you gain confidence targeting a publisher, read the next section. You'll find a practical exercise to do so that you can practice taking careful aim.

Beginner's Tip

If you submit a requested manuscript to a periodical publisher and they reject it, it's just part of being a writer. My manuscripts still get rejected even after an editor requests them. Try submitting a query with a different idea to the same editor, or just move on and find a different publisher to target.

Professional Track

You might land an assignment to write an article for a well-known and prestigious periodical. If so, try to pitch ideas on a regular basis with the hopes of becoming one of their regular contributors. Most editors build up a cache of favorite writers. When these editors need a certain article for an idea generated in-house, they turn to their regular contributors and offer them an assignment.

8.5 Target Practice

When I want to earn income as a children's writer, I look for a target publisher to send a query letter to. I zone in on one publisher, study their product line, and then pitch them a list of brand new ideas that fit their product line like a glove. If you want to earn income, too, you can learn to effectively target publishers and submit queries until you start landing contracts or assignments to write a manuscript.

Are you feeling overwhelmed with the thought of targeting a periodical publisher? How about this: grab your kitchen timer and set aside just one hour today for target practice.

First set your timer for 15 minutes. Use this time to practice choosing a publisher to target. Look in your market's guide. Pick up a favorite current magazine and locate the publisher's name. Skim publisher interviews in a current writer's magazine. Jot down the names of publishers you find. Don't stress out about it or take a long time doing it. Just look and find the name of one publisher who accepts queries and that sort of interests you.

Now set the timer for 15 more minutes. Use this time to practice finding out more about the publisher you chose. Search for their name on the Internet or go directly to their website. Look for their "submissions guidelines." Sometimes it's hidden under "About us" or "Contact us." If they don't accept queries, choose a different target publisher, instead. Print out any pertinent information you find.

Ready to move on? Now set the timer for 15 more minutes. Use this time to practice thinking of a way to break into their market. Read through a sample magazine until you find a filler or an article that you think, "Hey, I could try to write that!" Don't dilly-dally or reflect deeply into your inner soul right now—just skim through their features and note something that catches your interest. Jot down three to five ideas that could fit into the feature you're thinking of writing. For instance, if your target magazine features a biography of a famous scientist in each issue, list as many names of scientists that you know they've covered in the past year. Then list three to five scientists that you think they'd be interested in featuring in a future issue.

Now to reach the finish line. Set your timer for a final 15 minutes. Use this time to practice writing a query letter. Here's a sample e-mail query you can use—just fill in the blanks on this template and you're ready to go:

Dear _____ (first name of editor),

I read in _____ (name of magazine or website, etc.) that you are interested in _____ (type of articles they're looking for). I studied your website and see that you publish _____ (a feature they publish in their magazine). Would you be interested in receiving a proposal about _____ _____ (3-5 potential topics that would fit in this feature)?

Sincerely,
_____ (your name)
_____ (your contact info)

Here's how that looks in final form:

Dear Haley,

I read in the *Children's Writer* that you are interested in biographies for kids. I studied your magazine and see that you publish a biography of a scientist in each issue. Would you be interested in receiving a proposal about Einstein, Newton, or Marie Curie?

Sincerely,
Annie Author
123 Diction Street
Writewood, PA 12345
123-456-7890
www.annieauthor.com

Whew! You did it! All in just one hour. And if your target publisher accepts e-mail queries, it only takes one second to click the "send" button—and your query is on its way. If you send your query via postal mail, format it like a business letter, and be sure to include an SASE for their reply.

Beginner's Tip

If you don't yet have any published credits, just don't mention this in your query. Your eventual writing submission will speak for itself. Editors know every writer has to start somewhere. Many are willing to work with first-time authors, especially if they are open to accepting unsolicited queries.

Professional Track

Be sure to include your published credits in your query to catch the editor's eye and show you already have a successful track record as a writer.

Chapter 9
Target Books

9.1 The Children's Book Market

There is something wonderful, something amazing, and something extremely incredible about holding a book in your hands. If you've ever felt your heartstrings tugged by reading a book as a child, holding a children's book causes an even deeper sense of joy and wonder. If you know what I'm talking about, you're definitely a children's writer at heart. And you probably long to write a children's book, have it published, and see it held in the hands and captured in the heart of a child. If this is you, get ready for an adventure of a lifetime. You can learn how to target children's book publishers and lay the foundation for building a successful career as a children's book writer.

Part of the fun of starting out on this adventure is the preparation stage. To target a children's book publisher, organization is key. So let's get organized.

Purchase a five-inch expandable pocket folder to hold the papers for this project. Grab a handful of file folders to place inside the pocket folder. For starters, here's what to label some of the file folders:

- **Topics:** Start writing down ideas that pop into your mind for potential topics for children's books, and store them in this file folder.

- **Publishers:** This is the folder to collect information about potential target publishers.

- **Titles:** Start making a list of favorite books you find in the market you're targeting. Each time you discover a new title, locate it on Amazon.com. Print out key information about it such as the publisher, the year it was published, target age, and reader comments. Read the blurbs and reviews about each title to confirm information such as age range. Store this info here.

- **Notes:** This is the folder to store miscellaneous information you come across as you delve into the world of children's books. Store anything here that catches your interest and you don't want to forget.

Use a handy chart to organize your notes you'll be taking along the way. You can make this chart by hand or create a blank Excel spreadsheet. Make columns for: Publisher, Editor, E-mail, Website, Queries, Word Count, Titles/Year, Royalty/Advance, Print Run, % of First-time Authors, and Miscellaneous Notes.

Try to fit your chart on one page using landscape view or horizontal orientation for the page layout. Use abbreviations or small font to fit the title at the top of each column. Make your rows with enough height for you to write in. Place eight to ten rows on one page. Add borders for all the columns and rows, and print out your easy-to-use chart. Photocopy several blank charts and store these in a file folder to use as you need them.

As you explore, jot down key information on your chart as you go.

- Write the publisher's name under the Publisher column.

- Write the acquisition editor's name for the genre you're interested in targeting under the Editor column.

- If one is provided, write down that editor's e-mail under the E-mail column.

- Write the URL of the publisher's website under the Website column.

- Note whether or not they accept unsolicited queries or e-mail queries in the Queries column.

- Write the number of new book titles they publish each year in your genre under the Title/Year column.

- Under Royalty/Advance, write down whether or not they offer royalties or an advance.

- Under the Print Run column, write down the number of books they publish for a standard print run.

- Write down what percentage of first-time authors they work with under % of First-time Authors.

- Add anything else of interest under Miscellaneous Notes.

Because you're using a small chart for all this information, don't go into lengthy detail. Just jot down enough of a note in each column to jog your memory about each publisher on your list.

There aren't really right or wrong ways to search for publishers who publish children's books. It's more a matter of preference. Some of us would rather hold books in our hands, smell the ink, and flip the pages to locate the name of the publisher inside. Others would rather click, type, and search the Internet. Enjoy doing what comes naturally and what best suits your lifestyle. Most of all, just have fun. That's what writing kids' books is all about. Start by choosing one format to zone in on such as picture books, beginning readers, novels, craft books, kids' cookbooks, or educational books. Then grab your flashlight, a magnifying glass, and don your Indiana Jones' brown leather hat. Let the treasure hunt begin!

Market Guides

If you prefer browsing through your current children's writer's market guide, plan to read through the listings from A-Z. Sit down with your market guide in a comfortable chair. Explore the topical listings in the back, and read through the list of book publishers, jotting down key information on your chart as you go. Not every publisher will list every detail in your market guide. Leave those spaces blank for now.

Online Search

If you prefer the search and find features on your computer, go to Amazon.com to start your treasure hunt. Click on their Advanced Search option. (This is usually under the Books section.) Search for the key words according to the genre you want to write. Sort results by publication date and print out the results to give you a handy list of what children's books publishers are currently producing. Search by bestselling and print out the results to give you a list that shows what consumers are purchasing.

You can also look for children's books using your favorite search engines and searching for the same key words.

Bookstores

If you prefer a trip to your favorite bookstore, browse through current writer's magazines. Ask a store worker to point you to the section for the genre you want to target. Find as many books as you can, pick each one up, and locate its publisher. Get out your notepad and write down the names of all the various publishers you can find who are now publishing children's books. If a publisher's name sounds unfamiliar to you, be sure to jot down the address, too.

You may not realize it, but there are actually lots of publishers who aren't listed in the top writer's market guides. Why? They don't want to hassle with all those unsolicited manuscripts from wannabe writers who don't even bother to look up what kind of books they publish. Some publishers publish work-for-hire series, activity books, craft books, books for the educational market, or books to fill a unique niche. Many of these publishers don't list their contact information in standard market guides, as well. Since you're holding one of their books in your hands, however, and now know that they are currently publishing children's books, they might like to hear from you about a new book idea. You just have to work harder to find out their address, website, and contact information. Write down any contact info you can find about the publisher from inside the book, and plan on searching for them on the web when you get home.

Conventions

If you're planning on attending a convention such as BEA (BookExpo America), CBA (Christian Bookseller Association), IRA (International Reading Association), or ALA (American Library Association), and prefer doing your treasure hunt right in a publisher's booth, have fun. You can see and hold and read which children's books are hitting the markets *now*—even before they line a bookstore's shelves. Be sure to take lots of notes about which publishers are publishing what.

Libraries

If you love your local library, start your treasure hunt there. Ask your local librarian for help. Tell her you're a writer and on an adventure to write a brand new children's book—and you'll connect with an instant and valuable friend even if you've never talked with her before. Exploring your local library won't give you a current reading on brand new books coming out, but you will familiarize yourself with past publishers of children's books and be able to borrow these titles and take them home to read. After all, reading lots and lots of books in a specific genre is what writing a new book is all about.

Lists

Some out-of-the way places to look in your search for publishers is to look through lists such as in the Society of Children's Book Writers & Illustrators' (SCBWI) *Bulletin* where people announce their current publishing successes and awards. Look for titles of books in your genre, then make a note of the publishers' names if they aren't already on your list.

Editor Interviews

As anyone knows who is looking for treasure, sometimes the biggest prize comes from digging deeper. If you want to truly go for the gold, one of the best ways to find a publisher who is currently looking to acquire books in your genre is to find an interview with an editor who says just that.

If you want to dig deeper, look through the current year's past issues of writers' magazines such as the *Children's Writer*, the SCBWI *Bulletin*, the *Children's Book Insider*, the *Writer*, *Publisher's Weekly*, and *Writer's Digest*. Search for interviews of editors who say they're looking for the kind of books you want to write. Of course, this process takes a lot of time and doesn't promise guaranteed results, but if you can find such an interview like this, your chances of landing a contract and publishing a book increase exponentially. Why? Because you're not just targeting a book publisher, you're targeting a specific editor who actually explained his specific needs. This can make the difference between rejection and acceptance.

And of course, if you attend a writer's conference and an editor speaks and says he's looking for a certain type of book, then you've found the pot of gold at the end of a rainbow. Take advantage of this cutting-edge information and put this publisher at the top of your list.

If you're really adventurous, you can explore all of these different avenues and just have fun, fun, fun!

My, what a lot of work you've been doing! Congratulations on a job well done. It's as if you found the treasure chest and it's filled with valuable treasure. Now you get to reach inside and choose your favorite jewel or golden nugget. Read the next section to find out more about choosing one publisher to target.

Beginner's Tip

Look for publishers in your market guide who say they work with 40% or more first-time authors. These publishers are willing, and often expect, to train their writers on the job. What a great place to start building your career.

Professional Track

Even if you've received numerous rejections in the past from certain publishers, you can add them to your list of potential publishers today. You'll be approaching them in an entirely different way this time. Instead of trying to convince them to publish your manuscript as you did before, now you'll be contacting them about potential ideas that fit their product line like a glove.

9.2 Your Target Publisher

The world of publishing can seem daunting and overwhelming. It's easy to feel like a tiny little guppy lost in a great big ocean. If you take time to learn to know your target publisher, however, you can start to feel more at home in the publishing world. You can acquire a familiarity with one publisher, and then another, and then yet another. Each time you do, the "ocean" gets a little bit smaller. Eventually you'll feel like you're right at home swimming around in a cozy little pond.

Remember the Triple Crown of Success: Use separate strategies to meet separate goals. If you're targeting a book publisher for personal fulfillment, you can simply choose whichever publisher to target that interests you the most.

I don't recommend choosing a book publisher to target to meet your goal to get published, however.

If you want to get published on a steady and regular basis, it won't work for the children's book market because books can take years to finally get published and appear in print.

If, however, you are targeting a publisher in order to earn income, be sure you choose a book publisher who accepts queries. By landing the contract before you write the book, you can earn income while you're writing.

Look over the publishers you listed on your chart. Choose one that will help you meet your goals and interests you the most. Hip, hip hooray! This is your target publisher.

Now you're ready to spend time taking an in-depth look at your target publisher. Browse the publisher's website. Start with their home page. Identify links to visit for their children's books. Many publishers have various imprints, or different names, for different lines of books. If this is the case with your target publisher, print out the list of these imprints. Be sure to check them out before you're done.

Follow the links to learn more about the company in general. Is this a publisher that you could fit into? Do they publish books you might not want your name associated with? Does their platform look like a good fit for you personally and professionally? Explore their website as much as possible to get an overall, general introduction to their house.

Look for their "submissions guidelines" or "writers guidelines." Sometimes these are hidden under a link that says "Contact Us" or "About Us."

Once you find these, read them carefully to find out important information you need to know such as whether they require an agented submission or if they are open to receiving unsolicited submissions. See if they list the terms they offer—royalties and advances? Or only work-for-hire contracts? Note the word count they prefer for their books if they list this. Compare this information you find on their website with the information you already wrote down on your chart. Update the information to match the website. A website often reflects changes that occurred after the market guide went to print.

Explore your target publisher's list of authors. Do they only publish famous celebrities? Or does it look like they have first-time authors, too? Ask yourself how you would fit into the authors they like to publish.

Look at their catalog. Read the blurbs that describe their newest books. While you browse, jot down any ideas about anything that comes to you. Do they have series where all the books are written by the same author? This tells you that they might want to receive a proposal for a series of books rather than a stand-alone title. Do they have series where each book is written by a different author? This shows you that they might be open to a pitch about a topic not yet covered in that series.

Does your target publisher list titles of books front and center in their catalog that they published several years ago? This tells you that they might be great at keeping their titles in print for a long time. If they don't offer many books in their catalog written longer than three or five years ago, this tells you that your own book might go out of print very quickly with this publisher. This might not be something you want to have happen if at all possible at this point in your career. On the other hand, some publishers make it a practice to produce a lot of titles each year and let them go quickly out of print as new titles are added to their list. Sometimes it's easier to break into this publishing house because they're always looking for new material.

As you're exploring the website, note any books you see that you find yourself saying, "I think I could write that!" If you see titles that you feel would be way out of your field of interest or expertise, just move on and look for different books.

As you're exploring the website, you actually might find something that you really don't like about this publisher. That's okay. Just start at the beginning again and choose a different publisher to target.

Once you've studied your target publisher and feel like you know them fairly well, you're ready to choose potential topics for a book that you'd like to write about. Read the next section to find out how this is done.

Beginner's Tip

Don't feel like you're less of a writer if you want to target a small publisher first. I've written many of my books with small publishing houses and the benefits can far outweigh the money or prestige. Small publishers often welcome first-time authors, can be very personable, and often keep their titles in print for a long time. These are things that the big houses sometimes can't do—simply because they're so big.

Professional Track

If you don't yet have an agent and are interested in targeting a publisher who only takes agented submissions, check the websites of various agents who represent children's book authors. See which publishing houses their clients have been published with. If your target publisher is on their list, plan on targeting this agent instead of the publisher. Try to land a contract with the agency to represent your potential book. If they acquire you and offer to represent you, they'll work to help you get connected with the right publishing house.

9.3 Choose Potential Topics

Are you enjoying the journey? Do you feel like you're catching the vision and pursuing your dreams? Each step that you're taking is helping you establish a solid foundation for building a successful career as a children's writer. You can reach for the stars.

Now that you've studied your target publisher, it's time to choose potential topics. The best way to choose a topic is to study the publisher's current catalog and back list. Look at the books they already do. Which of their books interest you the most?

For example, when I studied one publisher's product list, I saw that they had several common groupings in their picture books:

- Folktales
- Animal stories
- Retelling of well-known rhymes or songs
- Rhymed stories
- Rhymed nonfiction
- Nonfiction

I decided that I liked their animal stories and wanted to choose a topic that would fit into that specific line. After I narrowed it down to the animal stories, I studied those particular books to see which topics they already covered and which ones they didn't. I made a list of the topics they covered and wrote down ideas for topics they didn't already have.

As you're on your journey to choose a topic, look for a potential series or set you can plug into. For instance, if they do a series of books on community helpers, you could try to think of a community helper they haven't yet covered. Or if they do a series of alphabet books, you could try to think of a topic they haven't yet published on their list. Just be sure to look for a series that is written by various authors. Don't try to break into a series written by just one author because chances are that the author is under contract to write the entire series himself.

The reason it's to your advantage to choose a topic that fits into an established series is because the publisher already has experienced a measure of success with that series. Certain libraries, schools, museums or other customers are already buying the previous books in that series, so they'll probably purchase your new book, as well. Plus, the publisher is already investing a lot of money into marketing that series. Let the publisher's success become your success. Learn to take advantage of any opportunity you can.

After you've chosen your main topic, choose three to five other potential topics from your notes, as well. It's always good to have a back-up at each step of the way in case you hit a dead-end. Once you've got your list, you're ready to move on. Read the following section to find out what's next.

Beginner's Tip

Go ahead and choose a topic that might fit into a publisher's list even if that topic isn't something you know much about. As long as there are adequate resources available for research, you can find all the information you'll need to know to write the book.

> ## *Professional Track*

As you're choosing a new potential topic, give serious consideration to the possibility of writing on a topic you've already written about and had published. The more you can specialize in any given topic, the better your chances increase of landing your next book contract.

9.4 Contact Your Target Publisher

Even seasoned writers can feel nervous about contacting a publisher. It helps to picture an editor sitting in her office with a stack of unsolicited manuscripts on the floor next to her desk that is taller than she is. Many of those manuscripts have been submitted by writers who didn't bother to check the publisher's website and have no idea which focus or format the editor prefers. You have the advantage, however, because you have been spending your time carefully targeting your publisher. When the editor reaches your manuscript submission somewhere in that six-foot-tall slush pile, she'll see that you've been doing your homework and she'll take note!

Remember the Triple Crown of Success: Use separate strategies to meet separate goals. If you're targeting a publisher to write a book for personal fulfillment, you can skip this step if you'd like. Why? Because you want to write this book for the sheer joy of the experience. You're willing to wait perhaps years before you see this book in print because you know the competition in this market is a tough market to crack.

But if you're pursuing the goal of earning income and you hope to write this book after landing the contract first, you most certainly can try. If that's your plan, however, it's important that you stop in your tracks and send off a query to your target publisher.

If your target publisher accepts e-mail queries, always take advantage of this option. It's free. It's fast. And it usually brings a quicker response. In general, if I don't hear back from an e-mail query within two weeks, I send a second e-mail asking for confirmation that they received my query. If I still don't hear back within two more weeks, I move on to find a different publisher to target.

If your target publisher does not accept e-mails, go ahead and prepare a query to send in the mail. The standard wait time in this industry for a response to a query sent through the mail is three months. Since many publishers simply don't respond if they're not interested these days, you can assume that if you haven't heard back by that time, you probably won't.

While you're waiting to hear back from the publisher, be sure to start working immediately on a different writing project. If you goal is to earn income, you can target a different publisher with brand new ideas and send off another query. Then another.

Don't worry that they all might respond at once. If it happens, just schedule a workable deadline to complete the first contract. Schedule the second deadline far enough after that to give you time to complete the second manuscript. Schedule the third deadline far enough after that to give you time to complete the third manuscript. I often schedule my deadlines out over the year ahead. Editors are used to career writers having various deadlines already on their calendar. They'll work with you to plan a date that's convenient for you both.

If your target publisher doesn't request a proposal, and you'd still like to land a contract before you write a book, go back and start at the beginning. Choose a different publisher to target and study them until you're ready to send out another query. Keep this cycle going on a steady basis. Keep sending out very specific queries to each different publisher you target until you land a contract. This will help you start earning an income and help build your career.

Be sure to continue building your Writer's Pyramid so you can build a successful writing career. Spend time working each week pursuing all three goals. Write new material each week for the no-pay/low-pay market to build published credits. If you're not yet writing under a contract, spend time each week submitting a steady stream of queries to target publishers with specific ideas to fit into their unique product line until you land a contract to get paid while you write. And always devote a portion of time each week writing new material for a project for personal fulfillment.

When your target publisher requests a proposal, contact them immediately and thank them for their interest. Respond to them in the same professional way they respond to you—whether via e-mail or postal mail. Tell them that you'll prepare the proposal and have it to them within one to three months. That's a standard time frame to prepare a proposal.

Editors will expect to see a different proposal for each different type of book in the children's book market. Look on each publisher's website to see what information they want to be included in a proposal targeted to them.

Types of Proposals

Here is a general overview of the various types of proposals for each different type of children's book:

- A nonfiction picture book proposal includes a cover letter, a summary of the proposed book, an outline highlighting information on each page or about each concept, and sample text of one page or concept.

- A fiction picture book proposal includes a cover letter, a summary of the proposed book and a sample of your writing—either published clips or sample text of one to three pages of your proposed picture book.

- Beginning readers and chapter book proposals include a cover letter, a summary or synopsis of the proposed book, and sample text of three to five sample chapters.

- Proposals for middle grade and young adult novels include a cover letter, a synopsis of the proposed book, and three sample chapters.

- Work-for-hire books, activity books, craft books, or books for the educational market often require proposals carefully prepared according to detailed guidelines. Check the publisher's website and follow the submission guidelines they post.

To help you gain confidence targeting a publisher, read the next section. You'll find a practical exercise to do so that you can practice taking careful aim.

Beginner's Tip

If you feel unsure about sending a query to a publisher if you've never written a book on this topic before, try writing magazine or newspaper articles on this topic first to test your wings.

Professional Track

If your goal is to earn a steady income as a children's book writer, pace yourself to move quickly through these steps so that you can target a publisher, choose several topics that might fit into their product line, and send them a query—all in a fairly short time. Then repeat the process each day or week until you start landing contracts.

9.5 Target Practice

When I want to earn income as a children's writer, I look for a target publisher to send a query letter to. I zone in on one publisher, study their product line, and then pitch them a list of brand new ideas that fit their product line like a glove. If you want to earn income, too, you can learn to effectively target publishers and submit queries until you start landing contracts or assignments to write a manuscript.

Are you feeling overwhelmed by the thought of targeting a children's book publisher? How about this—grab your kitchen timer and set aside just one hour today for target practice.

First set your timer for 15 minutes. Use this time to practice choosing a publisher to target. Look in your market's guide. Pick up a favorite current book and locate the publisher's name. Go to Amazon.com and check out various publishers of your favorite topic. Skim publisher interviews in a current writer's magazine. Don't stress out about it or take a long time doing it. Just find the name of one publisher who accepts queries and who sort of interests you.

Now set the timer for 15 more minutes. Use this time to practice finding out more about the publisher you chose. Search the Internet for their name or go directly to their website. Look for their "submissions guidelines." Sometimes it's hidden under "About us" or "Contact us." Try to find out if they take unsolicited queries and if they welcome e-mail queries or if you have to send it via postal mail. Print out any pertinent information you find.

Ready to move on? Now set the timer for 15 more minutes. Use this time to practice thinking of a way to break into their market. Browse through the publisher's product list until you find a book that you think, "Hey, I could try to write that!" Don't dilly-dally or reflect deeply into your inner soul right now—just skim through their product list and note something that catches your interest. Make a quick list of topics they already cover along that line and then jot down three to five topics that relate to it but they haven't yet published. For instance, if you're looking at a line of nonfiction books about wild animals, list the animals they've covered: elephants, lions, cheetahs, etc. Then list three to five topics you don't see, such as tigers, hyenas, and boa constrictors.

And now to reach the finish line—set your timer for a final 15 minutes. Use this time to practice writing a query letter. Here's a sample one you can use. Just fill in the blanks and you're ready to go:

Dear _____ (first name of editor),

I read in _____ (name of magazine or website etc.) that you are interested in _____ (type of books they're looking for). I studied your website and see that you publish _____ (topics or series they publish). Would you be interested in receiving a proposal about _____ _____ (topic they haven't yet published).

Sincerely,
_____ (your name)
_____ (your contact info)

Here's how that looks in final form:

Dear Haley,

I read in the *Children's Book Insider* that you are interested in nonfiction picture books to use in the classroom. I studied your website and see that you publish a series about wild animals in Africa. Would you be interested in receiving a proposal about tigers, hyenas, or boa constrictors?

Sincerely,
Annie Author
123 Diction Street
Writewood, PA 12345
123-456-7890
www.annieauthor.com

Whew! You did it! All in just one hour. And if your target publisher accepts e-mail queries, it only takes one second to click the "send" button—and your query is on its way. If you send your query via postal mail, format it like a business letter, and be sure to include an SASE for their reply.

Beginner's Tip

Many beginners see roadblocks and consider quitting before they even get started. They look up all the familiar publishers and see that they only accept agented submissions. That's because these are the huge publishing houses who rarely work with first time authors. There is a huge list of smaller publishing houses that are eager to work with first-time authors, however. Just bypass those big names for now and look for publishers who accept queries and say they are open to working with first time authors.

Professional Track

If you are considering signing with an agent at this stage of your career, target agents along with publishers. I know a children's author who landed mega-book deals through her agent with just a query for a manuscript not yet written. Let your published track record speak for itself, and submit a query letter about a potential manuscript to agents who accept queries.

Chapter 10
Picture Books

10.1 Target a Publisher

Each type of children's book has different nuances and challenges. The picture book is one of the most unique and challenging of all. A picture book is an entire story containing all the essential story elements such as characterization, plot, setting, and structure. Yet it has to be boiled down into 32 pages of text with an unbelievably sparse word count of less than 1500 words. All this and it has to have pizzazz, sparkle, and kid appeal as well. Even though the task may appear daunting, however, there are practical steps you can take as a writer to learn how to get published in the picture book market. There are strategies you can implement into your daily routine to become a successful picture book author.

The steps I show you in this section aren't about the right or wrong way to do something. You'll find plenty of that type of advice at writer's conferences or in workshops. What I'm sharing is what works for me. And the first thing I do *before* I write a picture book manuscript is target a publisher. I search for one specific picture book publisher who accepts unsolicited queries or manuscripts (or agented manuscripts if you have an agent) and publishes picture books like I want to write.

Before you get started, though, it will help you to understand which types of books fall under the category of "picture books." Here's a brief explanation of the main types:

Board Books

Ideal for baby's hands, these books are made of sturdy pages, are 12 or 16 pages in length, and have few or no words per page. These usually offer work-for-hire contracts and are produced by a type of company called a packager who then sells the book to a publisher.

Novelty Books

These books have a gimmick or interactive element such as lift-the-flap or touch-and-feel. As with board books, these are usually published by a packager and mostly offer work-for-hire contracts.

Concept Books

These picture books teach one concept such as colors, numbers, or the alphabet. Many do not contain a continuous story because the concept is the thread that unites each page. Length can vary.

Fiction

These books are the typical, full-color, hardcover 32-page picture books that you find in your local library. Most have a story, plot, and characters that appeal to children ages 4-7 or 5-8. Typical word count is under 1500 words, but many publishers state their individual preference in their guidelines.

Nonfiction

These picture books can be 32-pages, with some being 48 or 64-pages long. Longer books can be targeted to an older audience, ages 8-12. Word count can be much longer in a nonfiction picture book, so it's important to check the writer's guidelines for your target publisher.

When I want to target a picture book publisher, the first thing I look for is a real live editor or publisher who states exactly what type of manuscript he or she wants. I search for editor interviews or publisher news in magazines or e-zines for children's writers. I attend writer's conferences that feature picture book editors as their speakers. I study the current issue of the *Children's Writer's & Illustrator's Market* by Writer's Digest Books and *Book Markets for Children's Writers* by Writer's Institute. I look for houses that publish books on topics that interest me the most. I also visit the local bookstore and browse through current books until I find one that interests me and that I can say, "I'd like to write a book like this!" I search for publishers on Amazon.com and JacketFlap.com. I look for certain types of picture books that interest me, such as bedtime books or nonfiction wild animal books, and see which houses are currently publishing these types of books.

As you embark on your search for a target publisher, write down a list of publishers that pique your interest. Study their websites until you find one that seems like it would be a match for the type of book you think you'd like to try to write.

Follow the tips and strategies I share in *Chapter 9: Target Books* to choose potential topics for your picture book.

Remember the Triple Crown of Success: Use three separate strategies to meet three separate goals.

If you're pursuing the goal of personal fulfillment, you can go ahead and move forward to prepare to write your picture book manuscript.

If you're pursuing the goal of earning income, stop and send a query to your target publisher listing three to five potential ideas that fit their product line like a glove.

I don't recommend writing a picture book to pursue the goal of getting published frequently and on a regular basis. Picture books can take years to get published because after the manuscript is written, an artist then has to have time to illustrate the book.

While you're working on targeting a picture book publisher, be sure to continue building your Writer's Pyramid so you can build a successful writing career. Spend time working each week pursuing all three goals. Write new material each week for the no-pay/low-pay market to build published credits. If you're not yet writing under a contract, spend time each week submitting a steady stream of queries to target publishers with specific ideas to fit into their unique product line until you land a contract to get paid while you write. And always devote a portion of time each week writing new material for a project for personal fulfillment.

Writing a picture book is a wonderful experience. It's a journey of a lifetime. Read the next section to find out more about how to make the most of this fun adventure.

Beginner's Tip

If this whole process feels overwhelming, break it into bite-sized chunks. Pretend you're going on a treasure hunt, and enjoy the exciting adventure. Draw a treasure map that includes each step to take. Reward yourself when you find the prize.

Professional Track

Search for a picture book publisher to target whose editors prefer e-mails. This usually means they're used to moving at a faster pace than those who still wade through the slush pile. You'll probably get more immediate results when you contact them.

10.2 *Enjoy the Journey*

So far, you've been making important preparations that are critical to the eventual success of your picture book manuscript in the world of publishing. You've been working hard doing important tasks so you can write a picture book and write it well. Soon...drum roll please!...you'll actually start to write.

In the meantime, make sure you're having fun pursuing your dream. Get a little mascot to put near your computer that will make you smile as you think about the picture book you're planning to write. Purchase theme-related stickers and make a scrap-book page about the journey you're taking. Type up your goals along with inspirational quotes and hang these in prominent places. Listen to favorite music from when you were a kid. Read favorite picture books that you enjoyed as a child. Reflect on what made these stories touch your heartstrings.

Rearrange your schedule and take a mini-writer's retreat so you have a solid chunk of time to make your dreams come true. Put pizzazz into your writer's life in a variety of ways so you get excited about writing a picture book all over again. Then move on to the following section of this chapter to take your next step.

Beginner's Tip

Even though a picture book is the shortest book there is, it is the toughest to write and write well. Be encouraged! You're taking giant steps in the right direction to experience success.

Professional Track

Keep a journal or scrapbook of positive feedback from editors for other projects. On gloomy days, pull this out and get an extra boost of kudos and encouragement to fire up your enthusiasm to write.

10.3 Determine Story Ingredients

If you're preparing to bake a batch of yummy cookies, first you gather all the special ingredients together. You want to make sure you have all the necessary items on hand to bake a recipe that will bring kids back asking for more. Likewise, it's important to gather the essential story ingredients as you prepare to write your picture book. Taking time now to ponder these ingredients and develop them more fully will help you turn out a delicious story when you're ready to sit down and write. Determining your story ingredients now helps guarantee that you can write a story that will bring kids back asking to hear it again and again.

If you're writing a picture book for personal fulfillment, follow along with the next steps to finish your preparations to write. If you're writing a picture book for income and heard back from an editor requesting a proposal for an idea you submitted in your query letter, these next steps will help you prepare a power-packed proposal.

For nonfiction picture books, the story ingredients will be different for each different publisher. Does your target publisher include sidebars on each page? Is there a glossary in the back? Study your target publisher's nonfiction books to determine the ingredients your picture book should have and develop them as needed.

If your picture book will be fiction, there are three main story ingredients: character, setting, and plot. Of course, other ingredients will be added later such as dialogue. For now, however, we'll focus on these important three.

Character

Armed with library research books, I flesh out character sketches for the main character and supporting characters, if any. For instance, in one of my picture book manuscripts, my main character was a raccoon. I used nonfiction books from the library to learn all about a raccoon's quirky personality. I discovered that raccoons are curious, so I made my character curious, too. I found that raccoons are attracted to shiny objects, so I gave my character a favorite toy—a shiny rock.

I also like to choose the names for my characters at this stage. Of course, these might change over the course of actually writing the manuscript, but I like to start out knowing who my characters are. I use the Internet and a baby book of names to choose names for my characters. If my story is current, I choose current names. A good source for current names is in the yearbook of a local elementary school. Or borrow a young neighbor's or relative's school yearbook and see what names kids are familiar with today.

Setting

Setting is a very important ingredient in a picture book. Even though you might not write about it in the words you use, setting will be everything when it comes to the illustrations. This ingredient, above the others, is what makes a picture book different from a magazine story. Something different has to happen visually on each different page or spread of a picture book that demands a brand new picture. On the other hand, a story in a children's magazine can all happen in the very same setting and the reader will be satisfied with one or two illustrations that show what the character looks like. Not so in a picture book. If your story happens all in the same place, you might have a magazine story instead of a picture book. Solve this problem by making your main character move from place to place throughout the story. Develop the setting so the story carries the weight of a picture book.

Choose the setting for your story so that it will enhance it. Try to visualize the world your main character moves around in. This will help you write the story more effectively.

One word of caution, though. Choose your setting for your story but be ready to relinquish this over to the illustrator after you submit your manuscript to the publisher. Professional illustrators know how to add ingredients to the setting you haven't even considered. Learn to appreciate their input and creativity. Their expertise will add pizzazz and help make your story a success.

Plot

Sketch out the basic plot of your story. Present the problem right away, have your main character encounter obstacles as he tries to deal with the problem, show your main character changing in a significant way, and then let your main character solve the problem. All this adds up to a very satisfying story in the minds and hearts of your young readers. You can determine the various plot elements now before you sit down to write the story. This helps you keep a tight focus during the writing process.

Beginner's Tip

All this information is mostly for you, as the author, to know. Much of it won't need to appear in your actual story, but is background information that you need to know in order to make your story a success.

Professional Track

If, at this point, you realize you have more of a story than will fit into the tight restrictions of a picture book, consider changing to a different format that will give you more room to develop it properly, such as a chapter book or middle grade novel.

10.4 Structure the Story

There is no other book quite like a picture book. There's something magical about it. A picture book is special in many different ways—from the story's beautiful intrinsic qualities that stand the test of time to the actual internal structure and layout of the completed book. The great news is that you can learn how to create a picture book that has the potential to join the list of beloved classics

If your picture book is nonfiction, it's best to follow the structure of the books your target publisher uses. Create a working outline of the entire book.

If your picture book is fiction, it's essential to structure the story arc and plot in a very specific way.

Refer to Eve Heidi Bine-Stock's book, *How to Write a Children's Picture Book, Volume I: Structure*. A successful fiction picture book has a very unique structure that makes it a picture book instead of just a story. Bine-Stock's book is a must-have to learn how to structure your own picture book so it sings.

One of my favorite ways to map out the structure of a picture book is to use the chart on page 114 of *Volume I: Structure* where Bine-Stock maps out the structure for *Strega Nona* by Tomie de Paola. It was one of my boys' favorite books when they were growing up, so I'm well- acquainted with the story.

I actually created a blank duplicate of Bine-Stock's chart on my computer that I use for each picture book I plan to write. (If you don't want to make a blank chart on the computer, sketch one by hand.) First I fill in any information I already know. Then I put my thinking cap on...what will be the midpoint and plot twists? What can I use as each pinch to foreshadow upcoming events?

One by one, I plug ideas onto my blank chart until suddenly, the story takes shape right before my very eyes. Already, I can tell that my story will be much stronger and much more exciting than if I had just tried to sit down and write the story first.

After you are satisfied with the structure of your story, you're ready to submit a proposal to your target publisher. Read the next section to find out how.

Beginner's Tip

Always feel free to make changes to your manuscript each step of the way as you continue your journey. Don't feel like your map or chart is written in stone.

Professional Track

A fun activity to do with your critique group is to invite every member to create a chart as you each build the structure of your own picture book manuscripts. Compare and contrast the results, offering suggestions and feedback for improvement.

10.5 Submit the Proposal

A proposal is a way of letting an editor know the entire scope of your picture book. It also gives the editor something he can photocopy and distribute to the other members of the editorial team to read as he pitches your idea. There are standard proposals editors expect to see for a picture book. In this section I'll explain what these are so that you can feel confident preparing yours.

If you are writing your picture book manuscript and plan to complete it before submitting it to a publisher, you do not need to prepare a proposal and can skip to the next step. If, however, you are trying to land the contract before you write the book, a proposal is essential.

For a fiction picture book proposal, prepare a cover letter and a synopsis. If your plot can be described in one short paragraph, feel free to include the synopsis on the cover letter itself. If it is longer, you can use a separate page. Include several samples of your writing. For instance, when I prepared a proposal for a story featuring children as the main characters, I included two stories I'd had published in a children's magazine so the editor could look at my use of dialogue and character development.

For a nonfiction proposal, you'll also need a cover letter. Instead of a paragraph synopsis, however, it's best to submit an outline of the manuscript. Also include actual text for one to three sample pages of the projected book. For instance, when I submitted a proposal for an alphabet book, I sent the editor a cover letter, an outline listing which key words I planned to use for each alphabet letter, and a sample page of text for one of the letters.

After your proposal is prepared, send it to the editor. If an editor accepts e-mail, always send it via e-mail. It's free and will go directly to the editor's inbox. If they do not accept e-mail, send it via postal mail. Include an SASE for the editor's response.

After you submit the proposal, start working immediately on another project. If you eventually hear back from the editor and he's interested in sending you a contract, celebrate! Do a happy dance around your living room. Call your family and friends. Play a game of fetch with your favorite pooch and tell him what a wonderful writer you are.

Then on to the next step. You're ready to write the book. The next section will get you started.

Beginner's Tip

The proposal gives your editor a good working knowledge of the vision for your book. An editor realizes that as you actually sit down to write the book, however, some of the elements may change.

Professional Track

Be sure to include a separate resume that showcases your published credits. As my list of published books grew, I created two separate pages for my resume. One listed the titles of my books, their publishing houses, and the dates they were published. The other page featured important news such as awards, sales numbers of best-selling books, and magazine credits.

10.6 Write the Story

By now, you've been working hard as a writer. You've been going through important preparations a picture book needs to undergo as you get ready to launch it on the road toward successful publication. You can sit down to write a picture book, and you can start today.

When I sit down to write a picture book, often I turn off my computer. There is something very organic and creative about writing a picture book—actually writing the words—and staring at the computer somehow seems to block my creative juices. So I grab a pen, paper, a stack of picture books, and the pocket folder where I've been storing all my files for my current picture book project. I settle into a comfy chair with everything close at hand.

First, I read through three to five picture books. These aren't just *any* picture books, however. These are picture books by my target publisher that are similar to the one I want to write. I read through what already works for this publisher in order to get my brain focused on the right track and ready to create with purpose.

If my picture book is nonfiction, I work on it in chunks. I spend part of my time in my comfy chair to encourage my creative juices to flow. I study my working outline and focus on one chunk. When that chunk is finished, I take my work to the computer and type it in. Then I'm ready to tackle the next chunk. Sometimes I like to take a break in between each chunk so that my writing is fresh and exciting when I sit down again, not just a recitation of facts which can be boring to a young reader.

If I'm working on a fiction picture book, I look at the chart or map I made for my story's structure. I start writing little scenes that could be part of the story. I don't worry how "good" my writing is at this point. There will be plenty of time for editing and revision later. All I'm trying to do right now is to communicate and write down on paper the story from beginning to end.

As you sit down to write your story, I want to encourage you most of all to enjoy this process. You might want to just write the first page today...or the last page...You might get so inspired that you write the whole story down from beginning to end in one sitting. Whichever you feel like you want to do, just start to write.

Spend time enjoying the journey of writing a picture book. Take time to bring your story to life by writing down words on paper. If you take a break from writing, carry the story around in your head, jotting down notes, words, phrases, and entire paragraphs that come to you. Take a notepad with you wherever you go during this stage of the process.

When you're ready to come back to writing the story, kick off your shoes. Curl up on a comfy sofa. When I work on a picture book, I like to be as comfy as possible so I can enjoy the creative process as much as I can. Often I'll sit on the loveseat in my living room to look out the window and watch the birds. My cat, Humphrey, always hops up on the matching couch and gets as comfy as possible. He knows we'll be there for awhile. He waits as I read through stacks of picture books before I begin my writing session for the day. He listens patiently as I practice reading portions of my manuscript aloud.

By the way, it's important to read your manuscript aloud as much as possible. Picture books are meant to be read aloud, so it's great practice to read portions of it aloud as you go. Humphrey always has a ready ear, even if it's folded over by the pillow.

Once you start the actual writing of your picture book manuscript, you may find all sorts of things pop up throughout your day that make it seem impossible to find time to work on it. The important thing to remember is: Take time to write. Make time to write. Prioritize your manuscript and carve out at least 15 minutes to work on it each day. If that's not enough to finish it, sit down at least one hour each day to write.

Don't put on your editor's hat yet, though, or you might get too frustrated. Just make it your goal to write the first draft of your picture book manuscript from beginning to end. There will be plenty of time to edit it later. If you get writer's block and get stuck for an idea, pick up Eve Heidi Bine-Stock's book, *Volume I*. Read through her examples of classic picture books. Pick up the picture books you're using as research. Read and reread them again. Then go back to working on your own manuscript.

Don't worry that it might not be good enough. Don't fret that it has obvious flaws. Every manuscript has flaws. That's why pencils have erasers and computers have delete keys. Just get the story written down from beginning to end. Then you'll have accomplished your goal. And finally, you'll be able to take the next step and start editing your first draft. Read the next section to find out how.

Beginner's Tip

After you finish writing down your story from beginning to end, if you haven't done so already, type your manuscript onto the computer. Create a new folder for each new project you work on, and name the current new folder with the title of your manuscript. Inside this folder, store all the files you create regarding this project. Save your manuscript file and name the file with the manuscript's title or keyword. Save this file with the suffix A such as Raccoon-A. Next time you work on your manuscript, save it with the suffix B such as Raccoon-B. Then file C and file D, and so on. By saving each version of your manuscript as you progress, you can go back and retrieve something you might have changed earlier.

Professional Track

If you have successfully published in a different genre, don't feel bad if a picture book feels like an awkward fit. Just as learning to ski is different from learning to ride a bike, you can learn to do both. It just takes time, concentration, and practice.

10.7 Put On Your Editor's Hat

After you've written down the first draft of your picture book from beginning to end, roll up your sleeves, put on your editor's hat, and begin the editorial process.

To edit a nonfiction picture book, I like to go over the text various times, each with a different color of highlighter and a pen. One time, I'll go over and fact check. If I find any statement that I don't have three resources to support it, I highlight it in one color and write a note to do more research. I go through my manuscript again with a different color and highlight grammar or mechanical mistakes such as awkward sentence structure, weak verbs, or inconsistent verb tense. I use a different color to highlight areas in the manuscript that might feel boring or unclear to a young reader. After working on these revisions and typing the corrections on my computer, I then print out a fresh copy and start the editing process over again.

As I'm nearing the end of the revision process for a nonfiction picture book, a question I like to ask myself as I work is, "Did I say what I really wanted to say in this section?" If not, it helps to tell someone else out loud exactly what I was trying to say. Telling a child works even better. Sometimes expressing myself verbally and interacting with someone else's reaction helps me get the words just right.

To edit a fiction picture book, I recommend using Eve Heidi Bine-Stock's helpful books, *How to Write a Children's Picture Book Volume II: Word, Sentence, Scene, Story* and *Volume III: Figures of Speech*. These are excellent resources to help you begin self-editing your manuscript and make it shine.

Follow the examples she provides through classic picture books and take time to go through your own manuscript with a fine-toothed comb.

For instance, Bine-Stock discusses the importance of each word we choose for our picture book story. When I wrote a bedtime book, I made sure to go back in and add as many bedtime and nighttime words and phrases as I could such as: yawn, sleepy, tucked into bed, warm blanket, settled into bed, moonlight, and moonrise. I wanted the words I chose to create a sense of going to bed. The words themselves create the atmosphere of my story.

I also took out any word or phrase that conveyed an image that I didn't want in a bedtime story. I didn't want anything scary that might scare the reader. I didn't want anything loud or boisterous or hip, hip, hooray! I wanted the whole story to have the soft feel of moonlight glowing in a quiet bedroom, so I followed Bine-Stock's books as a guide and went through my entire manuscript to make sure each word, sentence, and scene contributed to the success of my bedtime story.

After you've finished the entire first draft of your picture book manuscript, it's important to continue to work on it and work on it and work on it until it shines.

Writing a picture book is very similar to making a quilt. When I took my first class on quilt making, I started small. I made a little lap quilt. Week after week, I attended class and learned how to piece all the beautiful squares together to make a delightful design.

Finally, I had assembled the entire quilt top. What a sense of accomplishment that was. I thought I was done. At my next class, however, I learned I was only *halfway* done. Now I had to learn how to assemble the quilt with batting and a back. I had to learn how to stitch the quilt all together. It took me just as long to finish the whole quilt as it did to assemble the pieces of the quilt top.

And so it is with writing a picture book. Plan to take as long, if not longer, to edit and polish the manuscript as it took for you to write the first draft. One activity that can help you make your manuscript shine is to cut and paste the text of your story onto blank pages so you can hold it in your hands and read it like a real book. To find out how to do this, read the next section.

Beginner's Tip

If you find yourself dreading the self-editing process, make yourself an editor's hat. It can be silly or beautiful or decorated to match the theme of your book—whatever suits your muse. Wear your hat while you're editing to make it more of an enjoyable time. Also, finding a local writer's group can be a great place to get help editing your manuscript with feedback from other writers.

Professional Track

If you really want to write for the picture book market, it's to your advantage to join a picture book critique group. Since a picture book is so vastly different from any other book, even successfully published middle grade novel writers risk the danger of offering feedback that will only serve to butcher your manuscript, not improve it. If you don't know of a local picture book critique group, form an online group. You'll be glad you did.

10.8 Make a Dummy

Often I like to make a dummy, or prototype, of my picture book. I do not do this with the intention of submitting it to an editor, but for my own personal benefit. You can make a dummy, too. It really helps during the process of editing.

How can a dummy help? Creating a dummy of your picture book will help you know if your story carries the weight of a picture book—or if you have inadvertently written a magazine story instead. It will help you detect weak spots in your manuscript and isolate key parts that need to be worked on as you polish your manuscript.

Plus, it's important to know how to make a dummy. Why? Because for the rare time when an editor requests that you submit a dummy (as I have had several times) you won't panic. You will have had practice and will already know how to make one. Besides, making a book dummy can be a fun part of the process of writing a picture book. It helps bring 3-D dimension and life to your one-dimensional manuscript. It gives you a book you can actually hold and turn the pages as you read the story you have created.

Use a published 32-page picture book with numbered pages from your target publisher to follow as you construct the dummy. It will help as a point of reference because it is very easy to get mixed up and number the pages of your dummy incorrectly.

To make your own dummy, follow these steps:

1. Stack 18 sheets of typing paper.

2. Staple the stack along the left side to resemble a book.

3. The front page and back page are the cover of the dummy, just like the front and back of a picture book. On the front write the title of your picture book. Underneath it, write your name.

4. The inside of the first page is the inside of the cover of the dummy. Leave this blank.

5. The second piece of typing paper is actually page 1 of the dummy. Do not write a number on this page. Page 1 of a picture book is

usually the title page, so write the title of your manuscript on this page and write your name as the author.

6. Turn the page. The back of the title page is page 2 of the dummy. Do not write a number on this page. Page 2 of a picture book is usually the copyright page, so write the copyright notice followed by the current year followed by your name. For example: © 2009 Nancy I. Sanders.

7. The next sheet of typing paper is page 3 of the dummy. Write the number 3 at the bottom center of the page.

8. Turn the page. Write the number 4 at the bottom of the center of the page on the left. Write the number 5 at the bottom of the center of the page on the right. You are now looking at a two-page spread of pages 4 and 5.

9. Continue through the dummy and number every page from page 3-32. There will always be an even number on the left side of the two-page spread and an odd number on the right side. If you get confused, look at a 32-page picture book that has numbered pages and it will help you number the pages of your dummy correctly. For example:

4, 5

6, 7

8, 9

10, 11

12,13...

10. Page 32 will be on the left side of the next to the last sheet of typing paper in your dummy.

11. The right hand side after page 32 is actually the inside of the back cover of your dummy. Leave blank.

12. Check through the dummy to make sure you have numbered all the pages correctly from 3 to 32. Compare it to a 32-page picture book with numbered pages to make sure you have done it correctly.

Now that you have made a blank book dummy from sheets of typing paper, it's time to cut and paste the text of your manuscript onto the pages.

Once again, look at the picture books you are using for research while you target your publisher. Go slowly from page to page. Note how some pages have more text on them than others. Note how some two-page spreads have one picture that covers both pages, while other two-page spreads have a different picture on each page. There is a "weight" each two-page spread has in a picture book and every spread should carry equal weight throughout the book. Each time you turn the page, it should be another defining moment.

Also note how much text fits onto each page. The amount of text on each page in a picture book is crucial. It can't crowd out the picture too much. That's why most 32-page picture books range from a total of about 800 to 1500 words. (Each publisher may vary slightly as to their preference and of course nonfiction picture books can have a much higher word count.)

Don't just cut your manuscript text into equal portions and paste a different section on each page of your dummy.

It takes time...and thought...

There are different approaches you can take:

- You can refer to the story map you made when your plotted the structure of your book.

- You can print out your picture book manu-script, tape all the pages together into one long sheet, spread the sheet out on a counter top or on the floor, and use a pencil to divide the manuscript into different sec-tions until you have all the pages you need. Then you can cut out the different sections and tape each section onto the correspond-ing page of your book dummy. Use clear tape that can be easily peeled off and restuck.

- You can just take a pencil and go through your manuscript and draw a line between obvious scenes. Count the number of scenes you have and then subdivide them by drawing in new lines until you have the number of scenes you need to fit into your picture book. Then you can cut out the different sections and tape each section onto the corresponding page of your book dummy.

- You can cut out each separate sentence of your book manuscript. Then you can tape them here, move them there, and tape them again to the various pages of your dummy until it all fits.

Just a note: Most 32-page picture books start on page 3 and end on page 32. Some publishers number their pages differently because they include an Author's Note or Glossary. Be careful to adjust your book dummy to take that difference into account. The key is to make your dummy to match your target publisher's picture books.

So grab your scissors and tape. Cut apart your manuscript and tape the text onto the pages of your book dummy until everything fits into place.

After you have your manuscript text cut into parts and taped on the pages of your book dummy, it's time to go through and evaluate what you have in your hands.

This part can be tricky, but the wonderful thing about it is that each time you go through this process and write a brand new picture book, and then make a dummy, you'll get better at your craft. You can't help it—you'll just get better.

One year, various friends announced they were having grandchildren, so I sewed my way through making five baby quilts. As I was working on my fifth one, it suddenly struck me that my sewing skills had drastically improved from the first quilt I had made of the set. My stitches were straighter. My quilt blocks were neater. My design was more colorful. It just happened.

So it is with writing. The more picture book manuscripts you write, the better writer you'll become. That's why it's important to keep on keeping on and continue to work on more manuscripts after this manuscript is done.

For now, you're ready to hold your dummy in your hands and read it as if you were reading an actual book. There won't be any pictures yet. (It's important not to add pictures because that will limit you as you are trying to determine which pages of the dummy to tape which parts of your text to.)

As you read, stop on each 2-page spread and ask yourself the following questions:

- Should this 2-page spread consist of one picture that covers both pages? Or, should it be two separate pictures on the two separate pages with the corresponding text on each page? Or, should it be one page of text and one page of just a picture? (Each 2-page spread throughout a picture book should carry about the same weight as each of the others.) Move the text and tape it on a different page accordingly until it works better.

- Is there a strong enough change from the previous spread and from the next spread to create its own separate picture? Move the text and tape it on a different page accordingly. (If you move the text and it still doesn't present a strong enough change to create its own separate picture, you might have written a magazine article instead. Magazine articles only need one or two pictures throughout the entire story to satisfy the reader, unlike a picture book which demands a new picture with every new twist of the plot.)

- After you read the text on the current two-page spread, do you feel satisfied with what happened on this spread, but itch to turn the page to find out what happens next? If not, you may have divided up your text in either too small or too large of a chunk on this spread. Move the text and tape it on a different page accordingly to see if that helps.

- Even if one two-page spread has four paragraphs and the next two-page spread just has one word, does each two-page spread carry the same weight, or oomph, as the others throughout the entire book? If not, identify weak parts of the story and work to make each one as strong as the other parts.

Continue to read slowly through the dummy, page by page and spread by spread, stopping and asking yourself questions to evaluate each one. Try to evaluate your picture book dummy and compare it to a published picture book you've been using for research as you target your publisher.

If you attend a critique group with other picture book writers, share your dummy with them. Ask for feedback on how you divided the text and pages. Revise the dummy until it shines.

Take your time. Enjoy the journey. And most of all, have fun!

When you feel satisfied with the dummy, now you can take the next step and learn how to type your manuscript in Picture Book Format. Read the next section to find out more.

Beginner's Tip

Sometimes an editor will request a dummy, a mock-up, or a prototype of your picture book. They're all the same thing.

Professional Track

Because a picture book relies heavily on the illustrations to convey the story, sometimes the story you wrote simply cannot be understood without pictures. If this is the case with your manuscript, make a dummy. Draw stick figures and simple illustrations on pages where they're needed. Then mail the dummy to the publisher as part of your manuscript submission. (Photocopy the dummy before you submit it, and keep the original for your files.)

10.9 Picture Book Format

Once you feel you have a strong working picture book dummy, use that dummy to type your manuscript into Picture Book Format.

Again, you will *not* be submitting your manuscript in Picture Book Format to your editor, but it's an important skill to learn. Why? Because some editors prefer a picture book manuscript submitted in Picture Book Format. Other editors require it. That's why it's good practice to write a copy of your manuscript in Picture Book Format. If you target a specific publisher and find out they require a submission in Picture Book Format, you'll already know how it is done.

Once you have your dummy constructed, it's fairly simple to write your manuscript in Picture Book Format. Just list the pages and underneath each page, write the portion of text that appears on that page. Align everything to the left. For example:

Page 3:
Once upon a time, long long ago, there lived three little pigs.

Pages 4-5:
The first little pig built a house of straw.

Pages 6-7:
The second little pig built a house of sticks.

Pages 8-9:
The third little pig built a house of bricks.

Page 10:
One day the big bad wolf walked into town.

Page 11:
He knocked on the house of straw.

Pages 12-13:
"Little pig, little pig, let me come in!" the wolf cried.
and so on...

I've known many writers who attempt to write their picture book manuscript in Picture Book Format without first constructing a dummy and the results are disastrous. The page count is off, the structure of the story is amiss, and it ends up being very confusing. Take time to construct the dummy first, and then write it in Picture Book Format.

Beginner's Tip

A picture book written in rhyme should have all text aligned left. Don't center the poem in the middle of the page.

Professional Track

If you feel your picture book requires a very specific page layout, go ahead and submit your manuscript in Picture Book Format to show the editor how it works best.

Chapter 11
Beginning Readers and Chapter Books

11.1 Target a Publisher

The beginning reader and chapter book market holds a wonderful joy all its own. These special books, uniquely crafted for very young children who are starting to master essential reading skills, can hook young readers and give the precious gift of a lifetime love of reading. Beginning readers and chapter books give children the confidence to announce, "I can read!" Parents, educators, and therefore publishers, are constantly on the lookout for new titles. You can learn how to write for this exciting and challenging market by following several key guidelines.

At my last estimate, I've written over 300 stories for the beginning reader and chapter book market. From complete stories just one sentence long geared for children learning to read their first words to entire books geared for older readers, this market is filled with fascinating variety and ripe with opportunity for you as a children's writer.

Before you get started, it will help to understand a few key elements about this type of book. Here is a brief overview:

Beginning Readers

Also known as early, easy, or emergent readers, these books are written for children who are learning to read in pre-kindergarten up through second grade.

Some publishers extend their line of beginning readers to go up to fifth or sixth grade, as well. Books range from 32-pages to 64-pages in length, depending on each publisher's guidelines. Average word count is under 1500 words, although each publisher usually has a specific word count for each level in their beginning reader series.

A wide variety of reproducible mini-books can be found in the educational market with even fewer pages, depending on the target reading level. These mini-books can be stand-alone titles in full color, or can be a book containing a collection of reproducible black-and-white mini-books for teachers to photocopy and use in the classroom. Books such as these can be found at teacher supply stores or general bookstores that carry books for teachers to use.

Beginning readers have controlled vocabulary and specific readability levels. The goal is for a child to be able to read the entire book by himself at the grade-level each book targets. Publishers who publish beginning readers usually have specific guidelines writers are required to follow so that manuscripts fit into their unique product line.

Chapter Books

These books are written to help children transition into the world of reading middle grade and young adult novels. Chapter books are the bridge between beginning readers and novels. Books range from 40-80 pages in length. Average word count is from 1500-

10,000 words with short chapters of three to four pages each. Once again, however, each publisher usually has its own specific guidelines for each level in its product line.

Hi-Lo Books

These unique beginning readers or chapter books are geared to meet the needs of struggling readers in fourth through sixth grade. Hi-lo books have a high level of interest but require a low level of reading skills. For example, the topic they cover appeals to older elementary students such as the history of the Civil War or sci-fi adventures, but the controlled vocabulary and sentence structure is simpler and easier to read. Once again, different publishers have different guidelines for hi-lo books.

As you embark on your search for a target publisher, write down a list of publishers that pique your interest. Look for publishers in both the general market as well as the educational market. Because many publishers in the educational market aren't listed in a standard writer's market guide, the easiest way to find a more complete list of houses that publish beginning readers and chapter books is to browse through the books in a teacher supply store in your area or online such as www.lakeshorelearning.com.

After you have a list of potential publishers, study their websites until you find one that seems like it would be a match for the type of book you think you'd like to try to write.

Different publishers offer different terms. Some offer work-for-hire contracts where they purchase all rights to the manuscript and offer a flat, one-time fee. Others offer a royalty-based contract where the copyright is registered in your name and you earn royalties on the sale of the book. Still other publishers offer work-for-hire contracts to writers who develop a book based on the publisher's idea, and offer royalty contracts to writers who develop a book based on the writer's own, original idea.

If you can't find out which terms a publisher offers in a market guide or on their submissions guidelines, check the copyright page of some of their beginning readers or chapter books. (You can often see the copyright page of a title by using the "Search Inside the Book" feature on Amazon.com.) If the copyright is registered in the name of the publisher, this means they probably offer work-for-hire contracts for this type of book. If the copyright is registered in the name of the author, this publisher might offer a royalty-based contract.

As you study various publishers and choose the one you plan to target, it's important to know that there are guidelines to follow if you want to write beginning readers or chapter books. Read the next section to find out more.

Beginner's Tip

One of the best ways to get a good feel for this market is to sit down with an elementary-age child and ask her to read a beginning reader aloud to you that is geared for her target age.

Professional Track

If you are already published in other markets for elementary-age children, it might benefit sales of your other books to write beginning readers. Beginning readers are purchased by teachers and used in classrooms across the nation. This puts your name directly in the hands of your young audience who otherwise might not yet have heard of you. This is great exposure and increases author name recognition.

11.2 State and National Standards

The world of teachers and students and classrooms operates closely connected with guidelines known as Standards. There are State Standards, which educational experts put together as requirements for teachers in each grade level to teach within their state. There are National Standards, which educational experts put together as requirements for teachers in each grade level to teach throughout the country. By taking the time to become familiar with these State and National Standards, you can navigate more successfully within the world of writing beginning readers and chapter books.

Once you've chosen your target publisher, follow the tips and strategies I share in *Chapter 9: Target Books* to choose potential topics for your beginning reader or chapter book. Since these books are geared specifically to teachers and educators to use in the classroom, however, brainstorm topics that fit into the State or National Standards for your target grade level as listed on such sites as www.education-world.com/standards/.

Explore various websites that list State or National Standards. A general rule of thumb to follow is that most states use the standards developed by California or Texas as their guide. It also might help to ask a teacher friend for a copy of his school's standards. Often, these are more detailed and easier to understand than just trying to read through the official standards. You can also visit your local elementary school to ask for a copy of their standards. Explain that you are a children's author, and most will be happy to help you by providing a photocopy, perhaps for a fee to cover the expense.

A very practical way to brainstorm for ideas that fit into the State or National Standards is to first make a list of the standards in the general subject area you are considering. For example, if your target publisher publishes beginning readers with a science theme for kindergarten through grade four, then explore the standards for science. You'll find that teachers are expected to teach physical science to students at this target age including an understanding of light, heat, electricity, and magnetism. Write these down on a list.

Now make a list of science topics your target publisher has already published about physical science. You might discover they only have one or two books about electricity and seven or more books each about light, heat, and magnetism. Bingo! You could pitch your target publisher an idea for a beginning reader about electricity to help fill the gap.

Once you brainstorm for ideas based on the Standards, next try to think of a fresh new approach to take on a familiar topic. When I do this, it's helpful to search for beginning readers or chapter books already written on this topic. Read through these books and jot down notes about what's already been covered. Then find one or two general books for children or adults on that same topic. Read through these books and make a list of ideas that haven't yet been published about that topic.

For example, instead of simply writing about how electricity works, you could pitch an idea for a beginning reader book about ways different people use electricity all around the world. You've taken a topic that's geared for the State or National Standards but approached it using a fresh new angle.

Now that you've learned about the State or National Standards in relationship to writing beginning readers and chapter books, you're ready to move forward. Read the next section to find out more.

Beginner's Tip

This is a great market to write for if you have a teaching background. Publishers in this market actually prefer working with teachers-turned-writers because most are already aware of State or National Standards as well as the basics about teaching children to read.

Professional Track

Interview local elementary school teachers and ask them which new or current topics they'd like to purchase for their classroom library of beginning readers books. Share the results of your survey in a query letter and pitch ideas to your target publisher for potential topics to meet this need.

11.3 Determine Story Ingredients

Once you've found your target publisher, brainstormed ideas to fit into their line of beginning readers or chapter books, and developed a fresh angle to approach your topic, it's time to determine your story ingredients.

If you are writing nonfiction, use your target publisher's nonfiction titles as a guide to help determine which story ingredients they will expect to see in your manuscript. If you're writing fiction, the three main story ingredients in beginning readers and chapter books are character, setting, and plot.

Character

The key story ingredient in every beginning reader and chapter book is its cast of characters. Young readers quickly identify with the character in a book they can read all by themselves. That's why this market is ripe for series with a strong main character. Children love to read more books about the antics of their beloved hero or heroine.

In this market, characters are usually the same age as the reader. Real kids make great characters in beginning readers and chapter books. So do animals with human qualities such as a super-intelligent dog or a mouse who is a spy.

Elementary-age children are discovering the world around them, and their world includes developing interpersonal skills with other children as well as an awareness of and developing love for animals.

Setting

The setting for many beginning readers is firmly established in the real world of a child. Even stories in beginning readers and chapter books involving elements of fantasy or science fiction usually have the real world as its launch pad or frame of reference. A school, a public library, and other places within a child's neighborhood are perfect settings for a story in this market. Places that are naturally exciting for a child to go are also exciting when used as a setting.

The zoo, the ocean, and an amusement park are all great backdrops for a story.

As you're determining the setting for your story, try to think of a fresh approach or angle to incorporate into the plot. For instance, in one story I wrote for a collection of beginning readers used in an elementary school's curriculum, I chose the setting to be a public library. As I considered a unique approach, I decided to place the public library in Alaska. My main character had to hitch his dog to his dog sled and race across the ice and snow to return his book before the library closed, or he would have to pay a late fee. Adding a fresh angle to a familiar setting increased the tension and excitement in the story.

Plot

In a beginning reader or chapter book, the plot is usually very simple. It is one-dimensional. It goes from Point A directly to Point B. Unlike books for older readers, there aren't layers of plots and subplots to confuse the reader. Beginning readers and chapter books are developed to help young readers gain confidence in reading fluency. If they have to try to figure out complex plots at the same time they're trying to decode and sound out new words, they will feel frustrated.

Real situations in the real world of children can provide all the plot a beginning reader or chapter book needs. Catching the chicken pox, celebrating the

100th day of school, and getting a puppy are all examples of simple plots for this market. Adding pizzazz such as humor or adventure spices up the plot and keep your reader's interest.

Remember the Triple Crown of Success

As you are gathering your story ingredients, remember the Triple Crown of Success: Use three separate strategies to meet three separate goals.

If you're pursuing the goal of personal fulfillment, you can go ahead and move forward to prepare to write your manuscript.

If you're pursuing the goal of earning income and want to land the contract before you write the book, stop and send a query to your target publisher listing three to five potential ideas that fit their product line like a glove.

I don't recommend writing a book to pursue the goal of getting published frequently and on a regular basis. A book can take a couple of years before it's actually in print.

Be sure to continue building your Writer's Pyramid so you can build a successful writing career. Spend time working each week pursuing all three goals. Write new material each week for the no-pay/low-pay market to build published credits. If you're not yet writing under a contract, spend time each week submitting a steady stream of queries to target publishers with specific ideas to fit into their unique product line until you land a contract to get paid while you write. And always devote a portion of time each week writing new material for a project for personal fulfillment.

Beginner's Tip

Simple works best in this market. Instead of adding a more complex plot or cast of characters, add humor instead.

Professional Track

If you already write for a publisher that has its own line of beginning readers and chapter books, talk with your editor and ask for tips on how to break into this market at the same publishing house.

11.4 Controlled Vocabulary and Reading Level

There are certain guidelines publishers often require for writers to use in the beginning readers and chapter book market. With careful attention to detail, however, you can write successfully for this exciting and challenging market.

These books operate by using controlled vocabulary and reading levels. What exactly does this mean? A controlled vocabulary means that each level of book only contains words that a child is learning to read in her own grade level. For instance, a child in kindergarten learns to read sight words (frequent words they recognize when they see them) such as *the, and, be.* A child in kindergarten learns to sound out or decode simple words such as *cat, dog,* and *box.* A child in kindergarten could not be expected to read difficult words such as *wrestle, signature,* or *nuclear.* Likewise, a child in kindergarten can only read short, simple sentences such as "I saw the cat." As children progress in school, they acquire stronger skills and can read longer, more complex sentences such as "Yesterday, I saw the cat sitting in the window, and it was taking a nap."

Many publishers develop their own reading levels unique to their product line. Some publishers in this market use their own vocabulary list for each reading level. Often, publishers hire reading specialists to endorse their series of beginning readers or chapter books. Writers are expected to write books closely following the guidelines, vocabulary lists, and reading levels the publisher has developed.

Some publishers, however, don't have such strict guidelines in place but still expect writers to understand the subtle differences between each reading level. The *Children's Writer's Word Book* by Alijandra Mogilner is an invaluable tool to use as a frame of reference if this is how your target publisher operates. This outstanding book features vocabulary lists for grades K through 6. It explains what children are learning in each of these grade levels and how that influences writing for this market. It describes appropriate sentence length and complexity for each grade, as well. An added bonus is that it has a thesaurus and a list of synonyms for various reading levels.

The best way to write for beginning readers and chapter books is to carefully study your target publisher's product line. Read as many books as you can in the reading level you want to target. Count the number of words in each sentence, the number of sentences on each page, and list the vocabulary words each book uses. Compare your findings with the titles geared for the next higher and lower levels.

If you've heard back from your target publisher responding to your query, it's time to write a proposal. Read the next section to find out how to fine-tune a proposal for the beginning readers and chapter books market.

Beginner's Tip

Some struggling writers suddenly start to thrive when they delve into the beginning readers and chapter books market. Working within strict guidelines and the tight focus this market requires provide the formula these writers need for success. You could be one of them, so give it a try!

Professional Track

Look for a publisher with several series of beginning readers or chapter books and brainstorm ideas for a brand new series that complements the ones they already have.

11.5 Submit the Proposal

Once you've caught an editor's eye in this market, you want to prepare a solid proposal to flesh out your idea. In this section I'll explain how to do this so that you can feel more confident as you prepare it.

If you are writing your manuscript for personal fulfillment and plan to complete it before submitting it to a publisher, you do not need to prepare a proposal at this time and can skip to the next step. If, however, you are trying to land the contract before you write the book, submitting a proposal is a necessary step to take.

As with most proposals, you will need to write a cover letter. In the cover letter, rephrase your initial idea that you pitched in your original query. Chances are, the editor might not have that easily at hand by the time she receives your proposal. Also list pertinent published writing credits if you have any. Explain how your idea would fit into your target publisher's product line, including specific titles when appropriate. List the target age, target audience, projected word count, and reading level for your manuscript. Include a short paragraph for marketing that explains why an educator or parent would want to purchase this book.

When an editor responds to your query and requests a proposal, do not feel restrained to fit everything on your cover letter into one page. If the information is vital to the success of your idea, include it. Use as many pages as you need. Just be professional and succinct.

In a proposal for a beginning reader or chapter book, a synopsis of the entire book will help the editor catch your vision. If your proposal is for a beginning reader, the synopsis can be one paragraph and can be included in the cover letter. A chapter book usually requires a longer synopsis with a short paragraph for each separate chapter. This synopsis should immediately follow the cover letter. A proposal for a nonfiction book should include a short outline instead of a synopsis and should immediately follow the cover letter. If your proposal includes an idea for a new series, describe the overall series as well as three to five potential titles to launch the series. Include a short paragraph blurb about each one. This series idea should immediately follow the cover letter.

Usually, an editor will want to see samples of your writing to determine whether or not you can write for this challenging market. If you have not yet written for the exact reading level you are targeting, send a sample page or two of your projected manuscript. If you know your target publisher assigns work-for-hire projects for this market, you could also ask the editor for a potential assignment to use as your writing sample. The advantage of doing this is that if the publisher likes what you write, they may purchase the sample assignment as well as offer you a contract for your own book idea.

Once you have your cover letter, synopsis, and writing sample prepared, submit your proposal to the publisher. E-mail it if your publisher accepts e-mail. Otherwise submit it through the postal mail with an SASE included. After you submit your proposal, start working immediately on another project. A standard wait time for a response in this industry is three months. If the editor eventually replies and offers you a contract, hip, hip, hooray! You're ready to write the manuscript. The next section will help you on your way.

Beginner's Tip

If your target publisher has submissions guidelines, be sure to follow them very carefully as you prepare your proposal. Instructions listed on these guidelines should take precedence over my advice or other tips you've heard elsewhere.

Professional Track

Learn to include a separate paragraph in the cover letter of the proposals you prepare describing how your book will fit into the current market. List three to five recently published titles similar to yours, but clarify how your manuscript will be uniquely different. This helps convince the editor there is need for your book in today's market and that it will fit into a specific niche.

11.6 Write and Edit the Story

Whew! What a lot of work you've been doing to reach this point. Now you're ready to sit down and write. Stir up your creative juices, tap into your amazing imagination, and chase after your dreams. You can reach for the stars!

Get in the groove by once again reading several titles of your target publisher at this reading level. Keep your target publisher's writer's guidelines or the *Children's Writer's Word Book* handy for quick reference as you go.

If you're writing a nonfiction beginning reader or chapter book, follow the structure your target publisher already uses for this reading level.

If you're writing fiction, young readers like to read about kids their age or just slightly older. Choose one main character and a single simple plot. Since pictures can be crucial to help carry the story along in this type of book, include art directions in brackets such as [Note for art: Child is carrying a green parrot on her shoulder throughout the story.] In the world of publishing, anything written in brackets signifies that it's not actually part of the text but is for the editor's attention.

In beginning readers and chapter books, dialogue is a key element. This also provides lots of white space on the pages which can seem less overwhelming to young children mastering reading skills. Action keeps the reader interested. And of course, humor always adds spark to books for this target age.

Once again, each publisher is unique about its likes and dislikes. Some want real kids in real situations. Some like animals as characters. Some like books with a moral or character lesson. Some like stories that tie in with the State or National Standards. Write your manuscript to fit in with your target publisher's preferences.

After you finish your first draft from beginning to end, don your editor's hat. Snip and tweak until it's the best you can do. Then send it on its merry way to the publisher. If you've been working under a deadline, be sure to send it in on time.

Once your finished manuscript enters the publication phase, there is usually a rigorous time of editing and polishing that it will undergo. Don't worry if yours requires a lot of work in the hands of the publisher. It's just part of the natural process that takes place in the world of publishing.

Beginner's Tip

If you find that you like writing for this market, ask permission to visit local classrooms for the age level you're targeting. This will open up a whole new host of potential topics to write about and help you better understand the dynamics of teaching kids to read.

Professional Track

Check to see if your publisher is marketing your beginning readers or chapter books to local or national school book fairs. Most only operate with a deep discount to the publisher which means a lower payment to the author. The huge sales numbers, however, often make up for the lower royalty. Since these books are geared for the classroom, school book fairs get your books directly into the hands of your target audience.

Chapter 12
Middle Grade and
Young Adult Novels

12.1 Target a Publisher

The art of telling a story is what writing for middle grade (MG) novels and young adult (YA) novels is all about. If you've been bitten by the bug to write for this market, give yourself a pat on the back. In the world of children's literature, this market is the most read, the most purchased, the most publicized, the most taught about in conferences, the most sought after for new manuscripts, and the easiest market to break into of all. The tremendous resources to improve your craft and the opportunity for publication make this a wonderful market to write for. You can hop on board, join the fun, and learn how to write successfully and well for MG and YA novels.

Before you get started, it will help to understand a few key elements about this market. Here is a brief overview:

Middle Grade Novels

Commonly referred to as MG novels, these books are written for children in the middle grades at school—usually from fourth grade on up through junior high. Target age can be kids from 8 to 12 or even 14 year-olds. Illustrations are minimal, if at all, or will be limited to one black-and-white sketch per chapter. These books can range from 64 to 192 pages, depending on each publisher's preference. Chapter length is shorter for MG novels than for young adult novels and can include 8 to 20 chapters. Word count can be from 10,000 to 40,000 words, once again depending on your target publisher. Check your target publisher's guidelines for the length they like to publish in each of their series. Series is a key word. Most readers at this age will be faithful followers of their favorite series, although there are a few stand-alone titles.

The outstanding characteristic of a MG novel is that the topic and characters are what kids this age care about. They want to read about what's really happening in their real world. Emotions—fears, joys, and sorrows—are key, all placed within the framework of an upper elementary or junior high setting.

Young Adult Novels

In the publishing world, these books are called YA novels, but most kids know these as books for teens. Target age can be kids from 12 to 16 or even 18 year-olds. Page length varies from 128 to 300 pages or even longer, depending on each publisher's specific guide-lines. Word count generally ranges from 50,000 to 70,000 words or longer, once again depending on your target publisher. Again, because teens purchase and choose their own books, YA series can be big hits as well as stand-alone titles. Check which one your target publisher prefers or if they are open to either.

The outstanding characteristic of a YA novel and what usually distinguishes it from a very similar adult novel is the fact that the main character is a teenager who changes in such a way by the end of the book that he or she is more grown up. The main character matures in such a way by the end of the story that a problem or situation can now be handled more as an adult would handle it, whether or not that problem or situation was actually resolved in the book.

Genre

There is a wide variety of genres in this market to suit everyone's taste—reader, writer, agent, and editor alike. Match your interest with that of an agent or editor and you'll be well on your way to success.

Science fiction, fantasy, horror, mystery, folktales, fairy tales, adventure, historical fiction, biographical, religious, nonfiction, creative nonfiction, literary fiction, popular fiction, guys or gals series, and licensed characters round out most of the list.

This list can change as fresh, new approaches hit the scene. For instance, a trend to include poetry within the pages of a MG or YA novel has opened up a whole new range of opportunities for writers to explore.

Learn about the various genres, frequent an editor's or agent's blog to determine their individual preferences, and read often and well in the genre you plan to write.

Ghostwriting

As you embark on your search for a target publisher, write down a list of publishers that pique your interest. Be sure to study your market guide. Also browse through your local bookstore in search of publishers who aren't listed in the market guide. Some of these publishers of MG and YA novels produce series under one popular author's name yet hire ghostwriters to actually write the books.

Landing contracts for these work-for-hire opportunities can be a great way to learn the ropes and start a successful career in this market. These publishers provide detailed guidelines, or a story bible, which series writers follow carefully. If this type of structure appeals to you at this point of your career, dig deeper until you locate such a publisher.

A clue that you've found one is when you see so many new books in a series all by one famous author that it seems impossible for any one person to write them all. You're probably right. Look up that publisher's guidelines and see if they hire numerous ghostwriters to write that series. When an author becomes famous in this market and his or her books are in high demand, sometimes they simply can't write enough books fast enough. Ghostwriters are hired to fill in the gap.

After you have a list of potential publishers, study their websites until you find one that seems like it would be a match for the type of book you think you'd like to try to write. Once you've chosen your target publisher, follow the tips and strategies I share in *Chapter 9: Target Books* to choose potential topics for your MG or YA novel.

Remember the Triple Crown of Success

Remember the Triple Crown of Success: Use three separate strategies to meet three separate goals.

If you're pursuing the goal of personal fulfillment, you can go ahead and move forward to prepare to write your manuscript.

If you're pursuing the goal of earning income and want to land the contract before you write the book, stop and send a query to your target publisher listing three to five potential ideas that fit their product line like a glove.

I don't recommend writing a book to pursue the goal of getting published frequently and on a regular basis. A book can take a couple of years before it's actually in print.

Be sure to continue building your Writer's Pyramid so you can build a successful writing career. Spend time working each week pursuing all three goals. Write new material each week for the no-pay/low-pay market to build published credits. If you're not yet writing under a contract, spend time each week submitting a steady stream of queries to target publishers with specific ideas to fit into their unique product line until you land a contract to get paid while you write. And always devote a portion of time each week writing new material for a project for personal fulfillment.

As with any work of fiction, crafting a middle grade or young adult novel requires essential story ingredients. Read the next section to find out more.

Beginner's Tip

Query a publisher who works with 40% or more first-time authors. If they like your query and offer you a book contract, you can feel reassured. They are used to working with beginning writers. Some even have guidelines tailored to newbies like yourself. They'll work with you to create a winning manuscript.

Professional Track

If you've had success getting published in other markets, target a work-for-hire publisher to get started in this one. Fitting into someone else's structure with already developed characters could be just the boost you need to establish a successful career writing in this market, as well.

12.2 Determine Story Ingredients

You've got a great idea for a story. Now it's time to develop that idea and flesh it out so that it takes shape. Taking time to choose your story ingredients now will give you the building blocks you need so you can create a story that pulls your reader into the lives of your characters and connects their worlds in a powerful way.

If you're writing a MG or YA novel for personal fulfillment, follow along with the next steps to finish your preparations to write. If you're writing a MG or YA novel for income and have heard back from an editor requesting a proposal for an idea you submitted in your query letter, these next steps will help you prepare a power-packed proposal.

Characterization

One of the books on my writer's bookshelf that is helpful to develop characterization is *Creating Characters Kids Will Love* by Elaine Marie Alphin. It's important to develop the characterization of both main characters and minor characters throughout the entire MG or YA novel—beginning, middle, and end. These characterizations have an important job to do. They help move the plot forward or throw obstacles in the way each step of the book's journey. It's also essential that you make your characters likeable. Even minor characters and bad guys who are so over-the-top unique will cause your readers to like them or to like disliking them.

Here are some general guidelines to follow as you develop characterization. Use this as a check-off list for the characters you're developing in your middle grade or young adult novel. Not only will this take your book to a newer level of interest and excitement for the reader—it will hook you in as the author, as well.

Main Characters:

1. Make each main character 3-dimensional by giving them each three distinct, over-the-top and unique personality traits. Either make them likeable or make the reader like to dislike them—don't just give them random traits—make them appealing to the reader in some way.

2. Develop each of the main character's characterization throughout the entire novel including the beginning, middle, and the end.

3. Have each main character change or not change by the end of the book in a dramatic way and with purpose.

4. Use the unique characterization of each main character to either save the day or bring about ruin by either moving the plot forward or throwing obstacles in the way.

5. Create character-driven plots to add tension and emotion to the story and to keep the reader hooked.

Minor Characters:

1. Create a cast of minor characters, each with one distinct and unique personality trait.

2. Develop each of the minor characters throughout the entire novel including the beginning, the middle, and the end.

3. Use the minor characters to move the plot forward or throw obstacles in the way and add tension.

Voice or Dialogue

When voice or dialogue is written effectively, each character provides very revealing insight about his or her characterization through the use of dialogue. We can see clearly that each main character has his or her own unique voice or way of talking.

As I prepare to write each scene in my novel, I like to try an experiment. In my mind, I sit all my characters down together who will be appearing in the upcoming scene. I ask them a question that is important to the plot in my book. I ask each one of them the exact same question.

Often to my discovery, only one of my main characters has anything unique to say. The rest are just me talking through them. Bo-o-oring. I then work to develop each of their voices and give each character distinctive dialogue in the scene that reflects the 3-dimensional characterizations I'm developing for them.

As an example, let's sit down with several characters from the classic middle grade novel, *Charlotte's Web* by E.B. White. Pretend we're E.B. and are about to write the scene where they capture Wilbur the pig to put him in the crate so he's ready for the fair. Ask each character to answer the question, "Why should Wilbur struggle against his capture?" Here's how some of the characters might answer:

Charlotte the spider: It's important that Mr. and Mrs. Zuckerman believe that Wilbur is a special pig, but not a strange pig. A special pig still acts like a pig and struggles when being caught.

Templeton the rat: I don't care if he struggles. What do I care? As long as he doesn't step on my tail it doesn't matter to me what the Zuckermans think about Wilbur.

The Goose: Hurry! Hurry! Hurry! Run around, Wilbur! Run around! Pretend like you don't want to get caught, caught, caught.

Can you see how each voice is unique for each character? Their very own voice reveals their very own personality and characterization. The choice of words and the way they say it work together to define their role in the story. That's the importance of voice and dialogue. That's how you want each of your main characters and supporting characters to talk in your own middle grade or young adult novel.

Plot and Setting

The plot and setting are essential story ingredients for a successful MG or YA novel.

The setting gives a sense of place for each scene to occur. Choose the setting for each scene carefully. Make it do its job, but in as unobtrusive and natural a way as possible. Use it to create an emotion, move the plot forward, or increase tension. Weave the setting into the story so that it feels like a natural part, whether it's the backdrop for the entire novel or the intimate environment of one small scene.

The plot is a complex entity. It's easy to mistakenly build the framework of your MG or YA novel on top of one single plot. This constructs a story that is one-dimensional and flat. It leaves the reader bored and in danger of putting the book down for a more exciting read.

Try to create at least three main plots. Develop them and refer to them often throughout the book, so that they are still important at the end.

Create numerous, character-driven or action-driven subplots that are developed throughout the book and are resolved by the end.

All these plots and subplots work together in a novel to make your book exciting, filled with tension, and interesting to your reader.

Timelines

To help create prize-winning plots and settings, I like to draw a timeline. First I draw a blank timeline on a piece of typing paper and divide into about a dozen equal segments. Then I photocopy this.

I make a separate copy of the timeline for each of my main characters and track how they are changing from beginning to end of the story.

I make a separate copy of the timeline for historic events that happened either locally or worldwide during the era my story takes place.

I make a separate copy for the overall plots, subplots, and setting changes.

Then I tape all the characters' timelines together, end-to-end, from left to right, so I can see at a glance what is happening to each one of them on the same date. I fold it like an accordion so it fits nicely into a file folder in my pocket files for this project. I tape the historic events, plots, and settings timelines in the same way and store them in the same folder.

Now I can track the pace of the plot and story line as well as how each of my characters changes throughout the story. I plan to add to the timeline as I sit down to write each chapter or develop new plot twists. If I notice an area where there isn't enough change taking place, I can make something happen to cause the change. Also, if I find a place in the plot that seems slow, I can increase the action.

It helps to have all these ingredients available at a glance so that I can make my story as action-packed, tense, and interesting as possible. All these elements are what make a middle grade or young adult novel grab and hold the attention of its readers.

Beginner's Tip

Writing a novel can be a daunting task. Be sure to step aside from your novel each week for a small break to write short stories for the no-pay/low-pay market. Build your published credits while exercising your storytelling muscles and improving your craft.

Professional Track

Join or form a critique group that specializes in MG or YA novels. Once or twice a year, break into small groups of two or three members and volunteer to swap entire book manuscripts between meetings.

12.3 Submit the Proposal

Once you've developed the characters for your middle grade or young adult novel, outlined key plots and subplots, and chosen the setting, you have essential ingredients for building your story. Use these ingredients so you can prepare a proposal with pizzazz.

If you are writing your manuscript for personal fulfillment and plan to complete it before submitting it to a publisher, you do not need to prepare a proposal at this time. Read through this section, however, so you know how to prepare a proposal when you reach that point. Because an MG or YA novel is so lengthy, editors prefer to see a proposal before asking for the entire manuscript.

If you are trying to land the contract before you write the book, a proposal is essential. Prepare a cover letter that contains the original idea you first sent to the editor in your query.

By now you should be building up your writing credits getting published frequently in the no-pay/low-pay market. Include these published credits in a paragraph within the cover letter or on a separate page, depending on the number you have.

Referring to one or more titles or series of your target publisher, explain how your novel will fit into their product line. If you're pitching a series as well, include a list of potential titles for the first three to five books in the series along with a short paragraph overview of the entire series. Note the target age, target audience, expected word count, and number of chapters for your projected novel or series. Double-check the publisher's guidelines to make sure these numbers fit into their unique titles or series. Follow their guidelines carefully as you prepare your proposal.

Most publishers require a synopsis of your novel. Many want a chapter-by-chapter synopsis of the entire projected book. Don't stress that your manuscript might change when you actually write it, however. Editors understand this. They just want to catch your current vision for the book and share it with the rest of the editorial team.

Write the first three chapters of your novel and submit these in your proposal as a sample of your writing.

If you are attempting to break into a publisher as a series writer or ghostwriter for an already established series, before you write this sample, ask the editor to send you several sample books as well as the story bible to use for reference. You want your first impression to hit its mark.

Once you have your cover letter, synopsis, and writing sample prepared, submit your proposal to the publisher. E-mail it if your publisher accepts e-mail. Many do in today's industry. If not, submit your proposal through the postal mail with an SASE included. Mark it to the attention of the editor who requested it. On the front of the envelope in large letters write: Requested. This helps it avoid the slush pile since an editor has already expressed interest.

After you submit your proposal, start working immediately on another project. A standard wait time for a response in this industry is three months. Some publishers do not reply at all if they aren't interested. If you receive a rejection or don't hear back after three months, choose another publisher to target. Start the process again and send a query with a brand new list of ideas to a brand new target publisher.

If the editor eventually replies and offers you a contract, it's time for a celebration! Do a happy dance around your apartment. Call a writer friend and gush the news. Go out for a special dinner with your family. Journal about your precious moment of joy.

Now you're ready to write the manuscript. The next section will help you on your way.

Beginner's Tip

If an editor doesn't offer you a deadline and asks you to set one instead, be practical. Write a sample chapter. Determine how long it will take you to write the whole book at that pace. Allow time off for holidays. Add a couple extra weeks for unexpected illness or delays. Three months to a year is a reasonable amount of time to request to write an MG or YA novel, depending on its length, other writing commitments, and the research involved.

Professional Track

Develop a template for preparing proposals. Plug in information for each new project. It will make the proposal preparation process run much more smoothly and efficiently.

12.4 Write and Edit the Story

Oh, the joy of telling a story! What an exciting adventure you've chosen to pursue. Treasure each precious step along the journey. Sit down at your computer and type. You can write your story, and you can start today.

To help fire up your enthusiasm, rediscover the wonder of growing up, and obtain practical advice, surround yourself with favorite writing books for the MG and YA market. Explore new writing books as well. Read them and refer to them often as you write. Two of my own personal favorites currently on my writer's bookshelf help me hone my craft as a fiction writer in general. These are the *Guide to Fiction Writing* by Phyllis A. Whitney and the *Novelist's Boot Camp: 101 Ways to Take Your Book From Boring to Bestseller* by Todd A. Stone.

As you write, also read books by your target publisher that are similar to the one you're working on. This helps you find your own voice while fitting successfully into your target publisher's product line.

Because of the length of novels, learn to edit as you go. I like to start each day's writing session first editing the section I wrote the day before. This helps draw me back into the scene and also provides a continuous process of self-editing.

Develop your own self-editing checklist. Here's one to get you started:

- Does your opening paragraph have a strong enough hook to draw your reader into the rest of the story? This needs to continue in each subsequent chapter, particularly following a great cliff hanger.

- Are characterizations developed to make each person unique?

- Is each person's voice and dialogue distinctive from the others?

- Are main characters carrying more weight in each scene than the minor characters?

- Is every single story ingredient working together to either move the plot forward or throw obstacles in its path?

- Do the subplots work together to increase tension?

- Did anything slow down the forward progression of the plot such as: dialogue, unnecessary scene, too much background information, too many details in the setting, bunny trail where writing wanders in a different direction?

- Is the setting clear but not obtrusive?

- Are the five senses included? Sight, sound, smell, hear, touch?

- Is the level of interest on target for this age range?

- Does the chapter end with a cliffhanger?

Don't be afraid to cut, tweak, add, or change. A manuscript is a work in progress up until the moment it arrives at the printing press.

Just be sure to save each new major revision of your manuscript as a separate file. Back up your files daily. One system I use is to e-mail myself my manuscript at the end of each day. I set up an online e-mail address so that if my computer crashes, I can go online from some other computer and retrieve my most recent manuscript version.

After you finish your first draft from beginning to end, plan to edit, edit, edit. Take it to your critique group for feedback. Work on polishing it until you've done the best job that you know how to do at this time.

If you've been working under a deadline, submit your manuscript on time.

If you have been writing this manuscript for personal fulfillment, take time to study the markets and submit a proposal to the agents or publishers of your dreams. Start working immediately on a new project so that you make progress in a new direction during the time it takes to wait to hear a response.

Learn to view your book as a team effort. You wrote the story with the helpful advice from other writers whose books or articles you read, or whose classes you took. You edited your manuscript with the help of the members in your critique group. Once it's in the hands of an editor, it's time for the editor to join the team and offer his input and expertise. Be an enthusiastic and energetic team player. There will probably be suggested revisions you don't agree with. Discuss these professionally with your editor. Learn to both give and take during the editorial process. Work together toward the common goal of presenting a polished manuscript into the hands of your readers.

Beginner's Tip

If you'd like feedback on your entire novel at once, offer to exchange entire manuscripts with one or two novel-writers in your critique group. Meet by phone or in person after a month to discuss the strengths of each manuscript plus ideas for improvement.

Professional Track

If you like to write novels at a fast and furious pace, look for a publisher of popular fiction series. These publishers often need entire novels written in six weeks or less at a steady rate.

Chapter 13
The Business of Writing

13.1 Manuscript Submissions

Writing is a business. Publishing houses exist to generate a profit. Highly trained editorial professionals don tailored outfits, travel through rush hour traffic toward towering skyscrapers, and crank out long hours in their office cubicle each day.

Even though many writers enjoy building their creative career in the comfort of their own homes, sometimes still dressed in their pajamas, the queries and manuscripts we prepare for submission must be presented in a professional way in order to navigate effectively through the hallways of the business world. Knowing several basic expectations editors have, you can learn what it takes to prepare a professionally-polished submission that spells success.

Queries and Cover Letters

Queries and cover letters are very similar. The basic difference between the two is that a query is a letter sent by itself. A cover letter is a similar letter but it's sent along with a proposal or the completed manuscript.

Thanks to the age of e-mail, queries can be a lot less formal than in the past. If you're sending an e-mail query, simply address the letter to the editor by her first name. Include a short description of your idea or ideas and how each will potentially fit into your target publisher's product line. If you are sending the same ideas to different publishers, be sure to state, "This is a simultaneous query." Conclude your query with your full name, address, phone number, e-mail, website, and blog if you have any that are writing-related. One click on your web URL and the editor can get an instant overview of your writing credentials.

Avoid sending file attachments at this point since many editors won't open them due to potential viruses unless they specifically request attached files in their guidelines.

If an editor does not accept e-mail queries or cover letters, type it more formally. Use white typing paper only. No cutesy stuff unless you have a profes-sionally-designed letterhead.

Center your name, address, phone number, e-mail, website, and blog at the top. Use Times New Roman size 12 font, single-spaced throughout. It is the standard in the industry.

Skip down a space and align all remaining text on the left just like a standard business letter. First type the date.

Skip a space. Then include the name of the edi-tor and the publisher's address. (If you don't have an editor's name just type "Editor.")

Skip a space. Address the editor by his first name such as "Dear Bill."

Skip a space. Start the letter and separate each paragraph by a space. Don't indent paragraphs.

When the letter is done, skip a space. Type "Sincerely," and skip four spaces, then type your formal name.

Sign it by hand in the space above your name with a black pen.

Query and cover letters are very important. They're the first thing an editor sees and if one catches her eye, she'll pass it around the editorial team. Length varies—many of my e-mail queries are just one paragraph long yet a cover letter for a series can be two or three pages. Try to fit your query or cover letter onto one page if possible, but it is okay to go longer if your proposal or manuscript is requested, or if you're pitching a series. No matter the length, I like to include four points in my query or cover letters:

- a description of my idea or manuscript

- a reference to my writing credentials

- how my idea or manuscript fits into the publisher's product line

- details about the projected or completed manuscript such as: age of target audience, projected word or page count, and marketability

Résumé

When I first started writing, I didn't include any writing credentials in my query or cover letter because I didn't have any.

As your list of published credits grows from writing frequently for the no-pay/low-pay market, you can list these in a paragraph on your query or cover letter itself.

Eventually, it's nice to include a résumé with your query or cover letters. As a children's writer, this doesn't need to resemble a business résumé.

I include a header at the top center of the résumé with my name and contact information. In my header I also list any writing positions I've held such as Contributing Writer for a magazine or columnist. I also include my membership in SCBWI or other writer's groups.

In the body of my résumé, I used to just list the titles, publishers, and dates of publication. As these increased, I separated these into three columns.

The goal is to make your résumé simple yet comprehensive while being visually appealing.

Formatting Your Manuscript

There are different suggested formats for different types of manuscripts. Learn more about these by studying examples in current market guides and writing books such as the *Writer's Market* (Writer's Digest Books).

A general format I use for most of my manuscripts is to type my name at the top left of the manuscript. On the same line at the top right, I state the general rights I'm offering to the publisher: *Picture Book Rights* or *Book Rights* for a book. Or *First Rights* for a magazine article, *Reprint Rights* for a reprinted article, and *All Rights* for a work-for-hire agreement. I'm not too technical here since the contract will be more specific.

On the second line at the left underneath my name I type my street address. On the same line at the top right, I state the approximate projected word length or page length of the book just to give the editor a general idea.

On the third, fourth, and fifth lines (or more) on the left I include the rest of my address, phone number, e-mail, and website information. All of this is single-spaced and written in Times New Roman size 12 font since this is the standard in the industry.

I keep the same font throughout, but then double- space the entire rest of the manuscript no matter what genre or format it is in. This is a courtesy for the editor's eyes as well as a standard in the industry.

I skip down several double spaces from my contact information, and type my title in the center. Then I skip down a double space and begin the manuscript in paragraph style.

This industry has standards such as these that are important to know. The business of being a writer involves other key ingredients as well. Read the following section to learn more.

Beginner's Tip

Many writers stress out about writing queries, cover letters, and résumés. That's why there are entire chapters and books written about them. Try not to stress too much. Just study examples in market guides, take yours to your writer group for feedback, and do your best. Practice makes perfect. The more you write them, the better you'll get, and the easier it will be.

Professional Track

Create a template to use for queries and cover letters. Just plug in your specific information for each unique writing project and send it on its way.

13.2 Finances, Contracts, and Taxes

It's really much easier these days to launch a successful career as a children's writer than in years past.

Organizations such as the Institute of Children's Literature (ICL at www.institutechildrenslit.com) and the Jerry B. Jenkins Christian Writers Guild (CWG at www.christianwritersguild.com) offer individual tutoring and a variety of highly recommended services.

Groups such as the Society of Children's Book Writers and Illustrators (SCBWI) provide helpful information through networking, conferences, websites, and newsletters.

Companies such as Writer's Digest feature in their market guides actual examples of various documents, helpful surveys of payment scales, current author and editor interviews, and comprehensive facts on the nuts and bolts of the business.

Once you start getting plugged into the right resources, you can quickly find information you need to answer your questions about the career of writing for children.

Managing finances is an important element of any career. As a freelance writer, much of the responsibility falls on your shoulders since you're essentially your own boss at the end of each working day, no matter which publisher sends you a royalty check.

I highly recommend talking with a tax preparer who specializes in small businesses and is knowledgeable about laws affecting freelancers.

When I first started out, I tried to handle my finances on my own and ended up losing thousands of dollars. Then I found a trustworthy tax service. I learned how to itemize, keep careful records of every applicable expense, and maintain a ledger of my income. I learned about different tax brackets and how to manage my career to keep most of my hard-earned cash instead of turning it over to the government. Connect with a tax professional now. Don't wait until you're earning the big bucks. If you do, you'll probably find yourself losing big bucks when tax time rolls around.

As soon as you start getting published, you'll also find yourself signing contracts. No two are the same. I've got file folders filled with them, and each publisher's is different. Chock-full of legalese and unfamiliar terms, they are all scary and confusing, to say the least. The general rule I follow is not to sign anything until I clearly understand what I'm signing.

Don't make the mistake of assuming that signing a publisher's contract is similar to signing loan documents. The publisher knows what they're doing and these contracts are all the same, right? Wrong. I frequently call or e-mail editors when I receive a contract and have questions.

Here is a sampling of responses I've actually received, some more than once: "The contract guy is new to the department and used the wrong clause on your contract." "I forgot to tell them to change that part of the contract for yours." "We've told the legal department that this contract isn't right. They won't listen to the editorial staff, but perhaps they'll listen to an author." "This is a new contract for us, and we just found a generic one to use without realizing it didn't apply to this specific project." "The secretary was confused and sent you the wrong contract entirely." The list goes on.

Horror stories circulate among writers about the ones who signed contracts without understanding the terms. Don't join the ranks. When you get your first contracts, network with other writer friends and discuss the terms. Photocopy the contract, white out confidential information, and discuss the meaning of each clause at your critique group. Refer to *The Chicago Manual of Style* for information about rights and permissions. Search the Internet for trusted sites featuring contract samples and explanations of rights. After your own research, contact your editor and ask him to help you better understand the contract. If you still have doubts, contact an agent or professional writing service and ask if they offer advice on contracts for a reasonable fee.

If you don't have an agent, you might wonder if it's advantageous to acquire one. Will it help you better navigate through the business of writing? Read the next section to find out more.

Beginner's Tip

If you attend a conference that offers a workshop on contracts, sign up. Take advantage of every available opportunity you have to learn all you can about this important aspect of your career.

Professional Track

Many contracts feature a clause stating that you can't write books that will compete with the current one you're writing. If you specialize in writing about a certain topic, this can limit your career. Learn to discuss this clause with each publisher to word it carefully and avoid this pitfall. Discuss how writing books on similar topics can actually *complement* rather than *compete* with each other, thus helping to increase sales for each publishing house involved.

13.3 *The World of Agents*

If you pick up a market guide, one of the first things you'll notice is that a significant number of publishers take only agented submissions. Don't panic! Explore the benefits and disadvantages of working with an agent so that you can make the decision that's best for you at this point of your career.

I always recommend that every author first get published credits under his belt and learn how to sign contracts first on his own before looking for an agent. Why? Because, as strange as it may seem, when you acquire an agent, she is in essence working for you. You're her boss. So you need to know if she's doing her job efficiently and effectively. How can you know if you've never worked through the process of signing a contract yourself first? Just be sure that you only sign contracts that you clearly understand by following the tips in the previous section.

The next question you probably want to ask is, "But how can I get published if so many publishers require an agent?" It's easy. Just skip over those publishers for now. There are plenty of publishers who don't require agented submissions. In fact some publishers prefer NOT to work with an agent. These are usually smaller publishers. They like to work with first-time authors. They're optimistic that good talent is still yet to be found. They prefer a more hands-on relationship with their authors. They might not be able to pay enough to support both an author and an agent. Read through your market guide and list every publisher that takes unsolicited manuscripts. Those are the ones you want to target since you don't have an agent.

If you plan to write for the lucrative work-for-hire market, you probably also do not need an agent. There are many opportunities for children's writers to land work-for-hire contracts. Nonfiction series, library books for kids, and popular fiction series are just a few niches in this market.

These book publishers offer a one-time flat fee, usually in the range of $1000-$5000. They like to assign fast deadlines such as four to six weeks to write a book. Their contracts are non-negotiable because they purchase all rights.

I know career writers who prefer working in this market because they love the detailed assign-ments, the fast pace, and the instant income.

Bringing an agent into the loop can cause prob-lems. It takes more time to communicate between more people so it slows down the pace. Also, agents like to negotiate contracts, and the work-for-hire pay scale diminishes quickly when part of your salary goes to an agent who might have minimal or zero influence.

However, there are two main reasons an author should look for an agent. The first is because you have experienced a measure of success as a writer and are looking for someone to help manage your career so you can experience even greater success.

The second is when you feel your writing skills are now solid enough that you are ready to have your work published by the big publishing houses that require agented submissions.

When you reach this point in your career, you have two basic options. You can look for an agent to represent manuscripts on a project-by-project basis. Or, you can look for an agent to manage your career. As you embark on your journey, get to know various agents by reading their blogs. Study their websites and familiarize yourself with their personal interests as well as their clients. Attend conferences featuring agents on their faculty and meet for private appointments if offered.

Working with an agent can have its benefits. It's great to have a personal writing coach. It's super to have a partnership with someone whose business it is to know more about the legal side of writing than you probably do. It's wonderful to have the entire world of publishing houses open and available for your submissions.

Once again, however, it's important to always remember that the agent is working for you. It's a business relationship. Be sure that if you're working with an agent, he is representing you at your best and with your best interests in mind.

Beginner's Tip

Even if you're not ready yet to sign with an agent, go ahead and schedule a personal appointment to meet with an agent at the next conference you attend. The experience will help you when you're ready to make that future decision. During the meeting, make the most of your time as well as the agent's time. Be prepared to discuss your own career goals as well as the type of author the agent is looking to represent.

Professional Track

If you would like to break into a certain big publishing house, look for an agent whose client list includes major authors for that house. This means that agent already has established a successful relationship with the editors of that house and gives you an extra advantage if he decides to represent you.

Chapter 14
Ideas and Marketing

14.1 Finding Ideas

Finding the prize-winning, eye-catching, award-winning, and best-selling idea can feel like looking for a needle in a haystack. Plus, the competition is very fierce in the children's market these days. However, I've got good news for you. There are practical and simple strategies that you can use to find that pot of gold.

One of the questions I get asked the most is, "How do you find your ideas?" My husband is a teacher and this is also one of the areas students struggle with most of all. One strategy to help solve this dilemma is actually very, very simple. Keep an idea folder.

I actually keep two folders. One is just labeled *Ideas*. I randomly stuff any idea in here from any-where including photocopies of something I read, printed pages from a publisher's online book catalog, and notes I jot down on a napkin (think Harry Potter success story).

The other folder is more sophisticated. It's a pocket folder, actually. In it are separate folders for new manuscript ideas. Each idea has its own folder because each of these ideas is something I think has solid potential. Inside each of these folders I stuff all the notes I jot down about this particular idea.

If you don't have an idea folder of some sort, start one today. On blank days when you're not sure what to write, browse through your ideas and choose one to work on. It's a simple, yet very effective strategy to jumpstart your creative juices.

The main strategy I use to hunt for ideas is more complicated, but it is very doable and has brought me great results for landing contracts. You've heard me hint at this process all through the book, and the reason I'm mentioning it here again is because it's the single most effective method I use to find ideas. I read my market guides and writer's magazines to look for publishers who accept queries, and then I study their online book catalogs with purpose. (I also use this strategy to find ideas for magazine articles, but I study issues of the magazine instead of the publisher's book catalogs.)

In a nutshell, here's what I do:

- I look for patterns of topics the publisher likes to publish. I look for groupings or sets of books such as parent/child relationships, bedtime stories, alphabet books, craft books, or dinosaur stories. These sets can be spread throughout the publisher's catalog or grouped all under their own categories.

- I look for established series written by various authors.

- I print out these groupings or sets or series, or write down the list on a piece of paper. For instance, say you find a publisher who does holiday books about each state. Just write down which states are already published and you're ready to go.

- Then I brainstorm ideas that have not yet been published by this particular publisher and that would fit well into this particular group, set, or series.

A practical way to brainstorm ideas is simply to make a list of obvious topics not yet covered. For instance, for the holiday books about each state, the list would include all the states not yet covered.

Sometimes it's not that simple to brainstorm topics that would fit into your target list. Search the Internet for that topic, and explore the results. Read an encyclopedia article about that topic, and look for related words that would complement your target list. Look through the index of a book on your main topic. Indexes provide some of the *best* ideas of all. Every word is a potential idea related to your topic.

To find out more about researching a publisher's catalog, read the next section. You'll find tips on developing an effective marketing strategy to market your book even before you find an idea.

Beginner's Tip

Keep notepads at hand in multiple places so it's always easy to jot down an illusive idea that flits through your thoughts. I keep a small notepad and pen in my purse, car, fanny pack, kitchen, bedroom, and living room.

Professional Track

Take this strategy to the next level by comparing books on your favorite topic published by different publishing houses. Brainstorm ideas for the next cutting-edge title in the entire market.

14.2 *Piggy-Back Writer*

Every single writer starts out as an unknown. Even famous celebrity writers weren't famous when they started out. Unless someone is born to be the future king of England, everyone starts out at the beginning. So if you're a beginning writer, take note! Whether you're just getting started as a children's writer or have numerous published credits under your belt, there's an exciting and effective trick of the trade you can tap into to guarantee that your book experiences success.

Learn how to be a Piggy-Back Writer.

You see, most writers are a Lone Ranger Writer. I was when I first started out. As a result, some of my books went out of print even before I received my author's copies in the mail. Actually! Somewhere along the way, however, I stumbled upon an exciting concept. I learned how to be a Piggy-Back

Writer. As a result, I started seeing amazing sales figures for the books I write.

Here's the secret: Look for a publisher who accepts queries and publishes a series of books written by various authors where you think, "I could try to write a book like that!" I've talked about this approach all through this book, but I want to clarify in this chapter why this approach is so important.

When I was getting started as a writer, I found a series of activity books that I loved. These books were published by Chicago Review Press and all had a similar orange and black cover. They all looked similar and were formatted in a similar way.

When I saw those books, even though I had never written such a book before, I thought, "I could try to write a book like these!" So I brainstormed a list of titles that hadn't yet been published in this series. I submitted my query listing several potential ideas and the editor responded that she'd like to see a proposal for one of my ideas. *A Kid's Guide to African American History* was born.

Because the publisher was already producing this series, it already had a steady list of bookstore clients who purchased the books in this series to sell in their stores. These clients included museum stores such as the Smithsonian and large stores such as Costco. Because this was a series, the publisher already had a steady list of individual people who purchased the books in this series. These clients included people like librarians and teachers and parents. Because this was a series, all of these clients automatically purchased the next book of the series when it came out. It happened to be my book, and the book sold over 35,000 copies in its first month off the press.

Because the publisher was already producing this series, they were already investing a substantial amount of marketing into their titles. So when the next book in their series came out, they invested a substantial amount of marketing into that title, too. It happened to be my book. They gave me postcards, marketed my book a gazillion places, and eventually published it in its second edition so that all their clients could purchase it all over again.

I had piggy-backed on the success of the series so that my book became a success story as well. I had piggy-backed on the successful marketing strategy of the series so that my book was successfully marketed as well. I had learned how to be a Piggy-Back Writer.

I used a similar strategy to jump on board the great series of alphabet books Sleeping Bear Press publishes. The result? *D is for Drinking Gourd: An African American Alphabet* sold over 70,000 copies upon initial publication. By the following year the publisher brought it out in paperback as well. The success story of a publisher's series became my book's success story, too.

In haunting contrast to these success stories are the Lone Ranger types of books I've had published. Books based on my own idea. Books that had to stand alone by themselves. Books that had merit and value and quality, but did not piggy-back on the success of an existing series. These books garner poor sales. These books go quickly out of print. These books are soon pushed aside for other more promising titles in today's competitive market.

Now I always search for the next possible way I can be a Piggy-Back Writer. You can, too! Just learn to spot series or groupings or sets of books in a publisher's catalog. Brainstorm ideas for titles that fit into their series and have not yet been published. Query your target publisher with your ideas. If they request your proposal and you land a contract, then hunker down and write that book.

After you've finished writing the book and it's actually published, there are other marketing strategies you can use to help boost its success. Read the next section to find out more.

Beginner's Tip

It's especially important to be a Piggy-Back Writer as a beginner. Nobody yet knows your name, but if you can piggy-back on an existing series, your name will soon become better known.

Professional Track

Stand-alone titles can have more success if you write them for a publisher you already work with since their clients will be looking through their catalog for their newest titles and recognize your name.

14.3 Successful Marketing Strategies

Getting a book published is a wonderful experience. But getting it published isn't the end of the story. Now there's work to be done to help your published book succeed. Just as a tender shoot planted in the ground needs nurturing and care to survive the onslaught of snails, drought, weeds, and rabbits, a brand new book benefits from nurturing with successful marketing strategies. You can explore various types of marketing and choose which ones might work best for your book as well as for you, yourself, as the author.

Grassroots marketing can build a successful and steady sales increase of your title, one book at a time. This type of marketing can operate on a small scale but work toward big results. It's the type of marketing you can manage within your own budget, personal skills, and time frame.

If you're already technologically inclined, one of the easiest grassroots marketing campaigns can start on your blog. A blog is a term used to describe a weblog, or website updated frequently like an online diary or news commentary. If you haven't yet entered the world of blogging, start taking a portion of time each week to set up a blog. Do some research. Network with other writers to discover which blog companies they use and why. Make a list of positive and negative services each provides, then choose the one that fits your needs the most. Personally, I like Wordpress.com. It's the blog company I use because it allows me to post blogs to appear automatically at a future date, it offers designs that also look like a website, and it's free. These issues were important to me as I was making my choice.

Market your books on your blog. Prepare a book trailer to advertise your book. Make separate tabs on your blog for each book or make a tab for new releases. Explore other writers' blogs and see how they market their books. Link to other, similar blogs and ask them to link to yours. Go a step further and plug into some of the many online blogging and networking communities. Target communities whose readership would be interested in reading your book, as well.

Host a Virtual Book Tour on your blog. It's quite pricey to hire a company to run the tour, so if your publisher isn't paying for this, set up your own. Plan interactive features to include on your tour. This gets online guests checking back in each day to join the fun. Games, contests and prizes are great incentives for people to participate on your tour. Just don't offer your book as a prize or everyone might wait to see if they won—and not purchase your book. Offer complementary prizes like a calendar based on the theme of your book or a small toy that ties into your topic. To find a variety of interactive features to include on your tour, check out other authors' sites to see how they succeeded. Search the Internet for "Virtual Book Tour" and have fun exploring.

Determine what you want to do on various days of your Virtual Book Tour. When I hosted my first tour, I decided I wanted to make mine a combination of:

- Links to other sites that feature an author interview they posted of my book

- Interviews of the illustrator, including samples of the book's art posted on my site

- Some all-text answers to questions students/teachers/librarians sent to me

- Short video clips taken in my home where I answered interview questions sent to me by people who read my book

After determining the ingredients of your tour, start making connections and spreading the word. Contact booksellers across the nation (both online and walk-in), other blogs who post author interviews, and websites that complement the theme of your book.

Explain how the tour will work, invite them to be a "stop" on your tour, and encourage them to check into your blog each day of the tour.

Don't forget to include your publisher on your tour. They might want to help spread the word, make important contacts, offer constructive feedback, and prepare press releases.

Other grassroots marketing strategies include doing book signings at your local school or bookstore. Tap into experienced writer's success methods by searching the Internet for "author school visits." Employ the methods that fit your personality, budget, and interest. You can do everything from hosting a volunteer storytime to organizing a power-packed assembly program complete with classroom instructional visits and pre-order forms for sales of your book.

To reach a wider audience, a great marketing strategy is to write articles for the no-pay/low-pay market whose readership would also want to read your book. Since your book is for children, local community freebie parenting and community news magazines can spread the word to thousands. Include your byline at the end of the article such as: *This article was written by Wanda Writer, author of Tasty Tidbits for Tots.*

Look for inexpensive companies to print business cards, postcards, and bookmarks, each with a full-color image of your book's cover. I'm always on the lookout for sensational free online deals that only require payment for shipping and handling.

Communicate with your publisher about your willingness to help market your book. Offer to prepare a promotional flyer if they haven't yet, and ask for their input on its design. Volunteer to prepare a teacher's guide with simple classroom activities if your book is geared for elementary age students. Your publisher might provide tips or offer to post this guide as a downloadable file on their website, as well.

Ask your publisher if they are submitting your book to various children's book awards. Book awards aren't just given out automatically. Each award-giving organization receives copies of books published each year to review as potential candidates, usually from the publisher. If your publisher isn't submitting your book for any awards, offer to prepare a list of potential children's awards for your publisher to submit copies of your book. Even if your book doesn't win, you'll know it was read and gained important exposure in the literary community.

Also, ask your publisher if your book might be a potential title for local or national school book fair organizations. Just a note—awards and book fairs frequently prefer to work with a book the first calendar year it appears, so be sure you follow through efficiently to meet their deadlines.

The limits for strategies you can use to market your book are only limited by your imagination. Once your book is published, make every preparation possible to enjoy this essential stage of its journey. You can nurture the sales of your published book, market it successfully, and reap the benefits of your hard work.

Beginner's Tip

Start marketing within your comfort zone. If you're shy, learn to use the Internet to your advantage. If you're technologically-challenged, set up speaking engagements to promote your book, instead. If you're both shy and technologically-challenged, sign up at your community center to learn how to improve your computer and public speaking skills.

Professional Track

Learn to start your marketing campaign when you start to write your book. Begin the process early so that by the time your book appears in print, you'll be well on your way to successful sales.

Chapter 15
Long-term Goals

15.1 Establish Your Authority

Setting short-term goals is mostly about pursuing the Triple Crown of Success and building your Writer's Pyramid. Day-by-day, week-by-week, and month-by-month, it's important to set short-term goals to help manage your time so that you can meet your goals of getting published, earning income, and writing for personal fulfillment.

Setting long-term goals as a children's writer includes all of that—and more. Setting long-term goals is helpful so your career develops over the years in the direction you want it to go. You can build a successful writing career as a children's writer. Establishing long-term goals along the way helps to guarantee your success.

One long-term goal I recommend is to establish your authority as a children's writer. You can start reaching for this goal today. Step up to the plate within various circles of influence with the plan of moving up the ladder as your writing career takes off.

For instance, you can volunteer to serve at local writer's conferences. Start within your comfort zone. Offer to help mail flyers for an upcoming event or sign in conferees on the morning of the conference. Continue to volunteer each year, taking on more responsibility as you become more experienced as a writer. Hopefully, one day you'll be invited to speak or lead a workshop, as I was recently for an organization where I've worked for years as a volunteer.

Get more active in your critique group. Volunteer to help in a capacity that you feel is manageable at this stage of your career. Be the timekeeper. Keep track of whose turn comes next each meeting. As your book career takes off, take on a higher-level task. Help manage your group's blog. Organize a fun contest for your members. Volunteer to help run the meeting if the leader is ill.

As you get more articles and books published for a specific genre, niche, or topic, organize mini-workshops with your writer friends to teach them how to succeed in this market, too. Volunteer to judge for a contest at your local or regional writer's conference. Join the staff of a manuscript critique service, then use your newly-acquired editing talents to offer private professional manuscript critiques and appointments at an upcoming writer's conference.

As you work to rise up the ladder of building your successful writing career by establishing your authority as a children's writer within various venues, people will take note. Other writers will start to look for your published works as examples to help them write their own. Name recognition will start to be established and your readership will automatically increase. Editors will remember hearing your name or seeing your face.

Establishing your authority as a children's writer over the term of your writing career has many benefits—one of them being that it helps you rise above the slush pile on an editor's desk. To learn about another long-term strategy that helps catch an editor's eye, read the next section.

Beginner's Tip

Another perk about volunteering to work at a local writer's conference is that they often let volunteers attend the conference for free. Sometimes they even host an appreciation dinner after the conference just for the volunteers—and invite the editors, too!

Professional Track

Many writers have stage fright. I do. I never could imagine myself speaking at a conference. But I knew it would help my career to include this as one of my long-term goals. So I started practicing mini-workshops within my comfort zone—at my local critique groups. Now I've done so many of these that stage fright is not the horror story it once was. If stage fright gives you the shivers, practice speaking within your comfort zone, such as your very own small group of writer friends. Gradually speak more frequently to larger groups until the day you feel you're ready to sign up as a conference speaker.

15.2 *Specialize*

There are important benefits for a writer who special-izes in a certain topic or market. Editors know they can trust this writer to successfully handle this topic on a child's level because of a proven track record. This writer can reuse research, which saves valuable time and energy. Readers look for other books this writer has written on a certain topic, and this auto-matically boosts sales. As a children's writer, you can make it a long-term goal to specialize on one or more favorite topics, and your career will reap the rewards.

After I had several books published, I realized I wanted to write more about certain topics. I decided to specialize in these areas. My three main areas of focus at that time included Bible stories, African American history, and beginning readers.

I began pursuing this long-term goal of special-izing by pitching new ideas based on research I'd already done. As these new ideas turned into more published books covering the same general topics, I then added more power to my pitches. I pitched new ideas to new editors, explaining in my queries that I now *specialized* in these topics.

The results included a significantly higher percentage of acceptance letters and a much lower rate of rejections. I landed more contracts more frequently to write more books even with publishing houses I'd never worked with before. Editors knew I specialized in the topics I pitched because I had the book titles on my résumé to prove it. My opinion carried more weight during the editorial and revision process. I felt more confidence throughout the entire process from pitching ideas to discussing contract negotiations to writing the book because I had written and published successfully on this topic before.

I collected key research books to add to my own personal research library. Then I used these same books over and over and over again for numerous different projects. This has saved me a lot of money since I'm getting the most mileage out of each reference book I've purchased.

If you decide to specialize, a few tips to keep in mind include maintaining a running bibliography of each research book you own. As you write new manuscripts using some of the same reference books, you can simply copy and paste the bibliographies from this file of the specific books you used into the manuscript for your new project. You don't need to constantly be rewriting bibliographies, which can be tedious work.

If you develop a simple code system for your reference books, it makes your work much simpler. For instance, I have one file that lists the title of each of my reference books. Next to each title, I have a simple code such as AA, AB, AC, etc. Each title has a different code. Then I pencil in that code in the front of the reference book that I own. When I work on my outline, I keep track on my outline of where I found each fact by listing the code of the reference book and its page number. For instance, AA213 means I found that fact on page 213 of the book with the code AA. This makes my research much quicker and more efficient than having to write down the entire book's title for each and every fact I use.

Since you're reusing your research when you specialize, you don't have to constantly start at square one. If I wrote about one famous person in one book and took detailed notes about him, I grab that folder or outline for my new book. I photocopy my notes from the first book, print out my outline and references for that book, and then put them all in a new file folder for my new project. What took me days and weeks of research for my first book only took me 15 minutes for my new book. And just like that I'm ready to start writing on my new project.

When you specialize, you do need to be more careful about the wording in the contracts you sign. Most contracts state you can't write another book that will compete with sales for the current one. I'm always very careful not to write a *competing* book, but I love to write books that *complement* sales for each other. An easy way to do this is simply to write for different markets or genres about the same topic.

For instance, I have a nonfiction book with historical-based activities covering African American history. I also have a set of middle-grade novels, an alphabet picture book, and a book of readers theatre plays all based on this same topic. Each reuses the same research but presents it in a totally different format. Each complements the other and doesn't compete.

I'm always up-front with my editors when I'm writing another book on the same topic. It usually involves a couple of phone conversations with my different editors at different publishing houses. I explain how writing both books on the same topic will help to increase sales, not compete with sales. I make sure editors at both publishing houses agree to this before I sign the contract. Usually, they reword the contract by having me write in my own handwriting above the competing books clause and initial it. They add their initials, too. The words I write usually state simply that other books of mine on the same topic will complement sales, not compete.

By making it a long-term goal of yours to specialize on one or more topics, your career will reap many important rewards. To learn how to take this to an even deeper level, read the next section.

Beginner's Tip

As you begin to experience success as a writer, consider specializing in a topic that interests you the most. Then target magazine and book publishers who are open to receiving queries on this topic. Start acquiring published credits to increase your credibility.

Professional Track

If you've been successfully published on a certain topic numerous times, when you pitch a new idea about that same topic, inform the editor that this is an area in which you specialize.

15.3 Your Magnum Opus

Every writer should have a magnum opus. I do, and it's changed my entire self-worth as a writer. You can have a magnum opus, too. It's a long-term goal that tugs at your heartstrings to pursue your dreams in a big way. It's a castle-in-the-sky type of project that captivates your imagination and helps you whistle while you work. It's the stuff of fairytales and dreams come true and wishing upon a star that every writer longs to have happen to them. Including a magnum opus in your long-term goals can add a sparkle of fairy dust to your long, industrious, and successful career as a children's writer.

Several years ago, I decided to write a huge, huge project that would eventually become the pinnacle of my writing career. It's way over my head as far as my ability or qualifications to write it. It's bigger than anything else I ever plan to write. But it's something I work on, word-by-word, week-by-week, and gradually it has become a part of me and is shaping who I am as a writer. It's my magnum opus.

I was inspired to create my own personal magnum opus after visiting the Getty Museum where I saw original paintings by the masters including Vincent Van Gogh. Van Gogh's story, especially, inspired me. Here was one of the greatest artists of all time—yet he felt little self-worth. In fact, because his paintings didn't sell well and didn't receive positive reviews, he ended up battling with depression and committing suicide. Yet his art is highly prized today.

As a writer, it's easy to feel little self-worth. Manuscripts are repeatedly rejected. Income can be sparse. People seem uninterested in something you poured your heart and soul into. All this is very much the same as what Van Gogh experienced.

I decided to pick a writing project to work on that I could pour out my entire creative energies into through writing—that was BIG, that would CHANGE MY WORLD, and that would leave MY footprint in history. It took awhile to decide on the project, but once I found it, I knew this was IT. I knew I could spend years working on this and feel that it was worthwhile in a big, huge way.

It started out innocently enough. I challenged myself to write an outline about a book that I wished every kid would have. You know—a classic—a book that would pass down from generation to generation and become known as a landmark among books.

That innocent little outline grew and grew and grew until after several months of working on it, it was over 150 pages long. I determined the projected length of my book—over 500 pages—and what I wanted to say in which part of my outline. Oh, I didn't know the exact words I wanted to write for each section, but I knew most of the topics I wanted to write about.

Since those intense months of writing my outline, I have been working on my magnum opus. Word-by-word. Paragraph-by-paragraph. I estimate that it will take me at least ten years to complete. When it's done, I hope to get it published.

But I'm not in any hurry. As a matter of fact, I keep my goal simple. If I write one hour per week on this manuscript, after an entire year, I'll have spent at least 52 hours writing and working on it. That's a bit, actually! And some weeks I spend more time on it than others.

I think every writer should have a magnum opus he is working on in between all the deadlines, contracts, manuscript submissions, and rejections. It helps keep me going. It gives me focus when other aspects of my writing career seem out of control. It propels me forward toward a worthwhile goal even on days when editors or critique group members inform me that rewrites are necessary on my other manuscripts.

I have chosen to "guard" my magnum opus from the eyes of the world until it is complete. I rarely take it to critique groups. I rarely discuss it with other writers. In fact, I work hard at making sure nobody has the opportunity to reject or criticize it. (I won't even tell you what my magnum opus is.) This frees me up to really let my creative juices flow. I try not to let myself worry that if what I'm writing is any good or not. I just try to say what I really, really want to say. I try to do the best as I can at this moment in time, and that's enough.

My greatest friend for my magnum opus has been and still is my outline. As I come across new information or get new ideas, I quickly open my outline on my computer and plug that information into the right spot. And when I eventually get to that spot, ready to write that page of the manuscript, I'll find that idea or bit of information there in the outline waiting for me. After several years of working on my magnum opus, my outline is now almost 300 pages long. It allows my project to grow over the years with me as I am growing as a writer.

And growing I am! Somehow, I'm different since I started working on my magnum opus. I feel a maturity as a writer I never truly felt before. I know I have self-worth as a writer. I know I'm doing something important. I know I'm working on something worthwhile.

You can experience the wonderful joy a magnum opus brings to the life of a writer, even while you're busy building a successful writing career. You can make your mark on history as a writer. You can write words that will change your world. Just believe in yourself, and you can go far.

Beginner's Tip

It might take years to think of a magnum opus. Just make it a long-term goal. Keep your antennae up and look for it as you build your career. One day, it will come to you. You'll know your magnum opus when you see it. By then you'll be ready to start.

Professional Track

Network with other professional writers to each determine your own magnum opus. Examine literature classics together. Discuss what qualities lifted these best-loved books above the others to stand the test of time. Brainstorm ideas together for what your own magnum opus could be.

15.4 Dare to Pursue Your Dreams

The most important long-term goal for a children's writer is to always continue to dare to pursue your dreams. Never give up, no matter how many rejections you receive. Always keep hoping, even when the market forecast is drizzly and filled with gloom. Never stop dreaming, no matter how impossible a task it seems. You can learn how to write children's books, get them published, and build a successful career. Yes! You can!

Just remember to move forward, one small step at a time. Do your best today. Then tomorrow do your best once more. Try not to compare or compete with other writers. Instead, share in the happiness of other writer's success stories. Meanwhile, set attainable goals to help yourself grow to become a better writer. If you do, one day you'll have success stories to share as well.

After you've finished reading this book the first time, go back and read and reread the chapters all over again. Each time you do, put into practice a little bit more about what you've learned. Don't just *read* about how to build a successful career—take action and follow the suggested steps so your career keeps moving forward in a positive direction.

Keep the Triple Crown of Success in mind as you choose which writing projects to pursue each week. Be sure to use three separate strategies to meet three separate goals. Write to get published. Write to earn income. Write for personal fulfillment. Just work on a separate manuscript and use a separate strategy to meet each separate goal.

Use the model of the Writer's Pyramid to help you manage your time. Focus your energy with careful time-management skills to maximize positive results for your writing career. Maintain a balance of writing for income, writing to get published, and writing for personal fulfillment each week to establish solid building blocks. You will reap the benefits and enjoy the rewards.

Always remember—you are a writer. You have a writer's heart. You have a writer's perspective. Put on your writer's glasses every morning when you climb out of bed. Look at the world around you with the delight and mystery and fascination of a writer. Dare to explore your world with imagination and creativity in tow. Dare to dream. Dare to pursue your dreams. In the wonderful world of writing for children, dreams still do come true. You can make them happen. Yes! You can!

Glossary

Acquisitions Editor:

Editor at a publishing house who accepts manuscript submissions from authors.

Activity Book:

Children's book featuring crafts, games, puzzles, or other activities.

Advance:

Money paid to an author before the book is published. Half of the advance is usually paid upon signing the contract, with the second half of the advance paid after the publisher receives and approves the completed manuscript. The advance is subtracted from the royalties once the book starts to sell. After sales earn enough to cover the advance, then the author starts to receive royalty checks.

Agent:

In the book industry, agents represent their authors, or clients, as they submit each client's manuscripts to potential publishers.

All Rights:

If you sell all rights to a publisher, this means that they completely own the copyright to your article or book and can use it however they wish.

Backlist:

List of books in a publisher's catalog that were published during previous years and are still in print.

Beginning Readers:

Also known as early, easy, or emergent readers, these books are written for children who are learning to read in pre-kindergarten up through second grade. Some publishers extend their beginning readers series up through sixth grade.

Blog:

Term used to describe a weblog, or website updated frequently like an online diary or news commentary.

Board Books:

Targeted to infants, these books are made of sturdy pages, are 12 or 16 pages in length, and have few or no words per page.

Booksellers Conventions:

Large conventions where owners of bookstores (also known in this industry as booksellers) gather to meet with publishing houses and purchase the newest titles to sell in their stores. Various conventions meet each year such as BookExpo America (BEA) and Christian Booksellers Association (CBA). Similar conventions are held for literacy professionals including the International Reading Association (IRA) and the American Library Association (ALA).

Byline:

Short sentence or phrase at the end of a published article sharing a tidbit of information about the author such as the author's name, title of her book, and website.

Chapter Books:

Books with controlled vocabulary and short chapters that form the bridge between beginning readers and novels.

Concept Books:

These books teach one or more concepts such as colors, numbers, or the alphabet.

Contract:

The legal document or agreement between an author and a publisher about the rights and terms concerning a manuscript. Both the author and the publisher usually sign a contract.

Copyright:

> The right to create and distribute your work. Every word an author writes is automatically protected under current copyright law until a contract or agreement is signed to sell rights to a publisher.

Cover Letter:

> Similar to a query letter, this letter is written to an editor and sent along with a manuscript proposal or submission.

Critique Group:

> A group of writers that meets to read over and discuss each other's manuscripts, offering helpful and constructive feedback for improvement or potential markets.

Draft:

> Any version of a manuscript at any stage of its development. The first draft is completed when the entire book has initially been written from beginning to end. The final draft is completed after the author has spent time editing the entire manuscript.

Dummy:

> A mock-up of a picture book, usually prepared by the author, that shows the projected layout of the text or illustrations of the book.

Educational Market:

> Books or materials published for teachers to use in the classroom, often written by authors with teaching experience.

E-zine:

> Online periodical with an e-mail subscription base.

First Rights:

> Also known as First North American Serial Rights (FNASR), this means that you keep the copyright for your article but give the publisher permission to publish it first.

Flat fee:
> A one-time payment offered by a publisher to the author for a manuscript.

Freelancer:
> Also known as a freelance author or freelance writer, freelancers work independently with a publisher on a contract-by-contract basis and are not employed or on a salaried position with the publisher.

Genre:
> A category such as science fiction, mystery, or adventure.

Hi-lo Books:
> These unique books are geared to meet the needs of struggling readers in fourth through sixth grade. Hi-lo books have a high level of interest but require a low level of reading skills.

Imprints:
> Names of one publisher's different lines of books.

In Print:
> Books that can still be purchased because the publisher is still publishing them.

Kill Fee:
> Fee paid to the author if a contract has been signed but the publisher decided not to publish the manuscript and offers a one-time payment, instead.

Manuscript:
> The work a writer is preparing on a word-processing program. The writer prints out this work to share with a critique group or mail to an editor.

Market Guides:
> List of publishers that includes contact information along with pertinent details about each one's unique product line and policies for dealing with authors.

Masthead:
> Section of magazine or periodical listing editors' names, authors' names, and publisher's information.

Middle Grade (MG):
>   Targeted to readers in upper elementary and sometimes through junior high.

Name Recognition:
>   When authors are so famous that people purchase their books or read their articles based on the recognition of their name.

Novelty Books:
>   These books have a gimmick or interactive element such as lift-the-flap or touch-and-feel.

On Spec:
>   When a publisher agrees to assign an author the task of writing a manuscript on speculation, but does not plan to offer a contract until after the manuscript is completed and approved.

Out of Print:
>   After a publisher determines not to print any more copies of a title, that book goes out of print when the publisher decides to stop publishing it.

Packager:
>   A type of company that produces books such as board books or novelty books and then sells the books to a publisher.

Picture Book (PB):
>   Books for young children comprising mostly illustrations or pictures.

Print Run:
>   The number of copies a publisher decides to print at one time, usually of a new book.

Proposal:
>   A submission sent to a publisher that generally consists of a cover letter explaining a projected manuscript, along with sample text of the project or a sample of the author's published work.

Publishing House:
> A corporation or business that publishes books, maga-
> zines, or other materials.

Query Letter:
> Similar to a cover letter, this letter is sent by itself to a
> publisher to ask if the publisher would like to receive a
> proposal or completed manuscript submission.

Rejection Letter:
> Letter sent to authors stating that the publisher will not
> be accepting their manuscript for publication.

Reprint Rights:
> This means that your article has been published else-
> where already, and you're giving permission for a differ-
> ent periodical to publish it once more.

Rights:
> Authors sell a variety of rights to publishers, giving the
> publishers permission to publish and sell their manu-
> scripts according to which rights are sold.

Royalty:
> The percentage of income from a book that is paid to the
> author by the publisher.

SASE or Self-Addressed, Stamped Envelope:
> Some publishers ask that a self-addressed, stamped en-
> velope, or SASE, be included with a manuscript submis-
> sion for their reply or for returning your manuscript if
> it's rejected.

Simultaneous Submission:
> A manuscript sent to several publishers at the same time.
> Authors are required to always tell a publisher if they are
> sending a simultaneous submission.

Slush pile:
> Term for the stack or pile of unsolicited manuscript
> submissions an editor receives.

Spread:

A term commonly used in the picture book market. A spread comprises two pages of the book, that when opened up, can be seen at the same time. A spread always has an even page number on the left-hand page and an odd page number on the right-hand page.

Story bible:

Set of specific instructions prepared by the publisher to be followed by the author when writing a new title for an established series of books.

Submission:

Manuscript sent by an author to a publisher or agent.

Submissions Guidelines:

Also known as Writer's Guidelines. Often found on a publisher's website under "About us" or "Contact us," these guidelines spell out the publisher's interests and how an author should submit a query, proposal, or completed manuscript to the publisher. Each publisher's guidelines are uniquely suited to its individual needs and product line.

Synopsis:

Overview of a projected or completed manuscript that is often requested as part of a proposal.

Unsolicited Submission:

Manuscript sent to a publisher without an editor's request.

Work-for-hire Market:

Publishers in this market purchase all rights from the author and usually pay a one-time, flat fee for the completed manuscript.

Young Adult (YA):

Targeted to readers 12 to 16 or even 18 years old.

Recommended Books for Children's Writers

Market Guides

- *Book Markets for Children's Writers* (Writer's Institute Publications ™)
- *Children's Writer's & Illustrator's Market* (Writer's Digest Books)
- *Christian Writers' Market Guide* by Sally Stuart
- *Magazine Markets for Children's Writers* (Writer's Institute Publications ™)
- *Writer's Market* (Writer's Digest Books)

Children's Writers' Books

- *The Complete Idiot's Guide® to Publishing Children's Books* by Harold D. Underdown
- *The Everything® Guide to Writing Children's Books* by Lesley Bolton
- *How to Write a Children's Book and Get it Published* by Barbara Seuling
- *How to Write a Children's Picture Book, Volume I: Structure* by Eve Heidi Bine-Stock
- *How to Write a Children's Picture Book, Volume II: Word, Sentence, Scene, Story* by Eve Heidi Bine-Stock

- *How to Write a Children's Picture Book, Volume III: Figures of Speech* by Eve Heidi Bine-Stock
- *Picture Writing* by Anastasia Suen
- *Writing Children's Books for Dummies®* by Lisa Rojany Buccieri and Peter Economy
- *Writing for Children & Teenagers* by Lee Wyndham
- *Writing Juvenile Stories and Novels* by Phyllis A. Whitney
- *You Can Write Children's Books* by Tracey E. Dils
- *You Can Write Children's Books Workbook* by Tracey E. Dils

Of Special Interest

- *35000+ Baby Names* by Bruce Lansky
- *Chase's Calendar of Events* (McGraw-Hill)
- *Children's Writer® Guide* (Writer's Institute Publications ™)
- *Children's Writer's Word Book* by Alijandra Mogilner
- *Creating Characters Kids Will Love* by Elaine Marie Alphin
- *The Complete Rhyming Dictionary* by Clement Wood
- *Guide to Fiction Writing* by Phyllis A. Whitney
- *Novelist's Boot Camp: 101 Ways to Take Your Book From Boring to Bestseller* by Todd A. Stone

- *Secrets of a Freelance Writer: How to Make $100,000 a Year or More* by Robert W. Bly
- *The Timetables of History* by Bernard Grun
- *Writing Skills Made Fun* series by Karen Kellaher: *Capitalization, Punctuation, and Spelling; Parts of Speech; Sentences and Paragraphs*

Manuals on Grammar and Style

- *The Chicago Manual of Style* (The University of Chicago Press)
- *The Christian Writer's Manual of Style* by Robert Hudson, General Editor
- *The Elements of Style* by Strunk and White
- *Rewrite Right!* By Jan Venolia
- *Write Right!* by Jan Venolia

Books by the Author

Nancy I. Sanders is the award-winning and best-selling children's author of over 75 books. She has been published by such houses as Scholastic Teaching Resources, Reader's Digest Children's Books, Sleeping Bear Press, Tyndale, and Standard. Please visit her website at www.nancyisanders.com.

Picture Books

- D is for Drinking Gourd: An African American Alphabet
- Easter (A True Book)
- Passover (A True Book)
- Earth Day (A True Book)
- Independence Day (A True Book)
- The Fall into Sin (Arch Book)
- Jesus Walks on Water (Arch Book)

Board Books and Novelty Books

- The Pet I'll Get
- My Many Hats
- My Special Things
- Can't Catch Me
- Off to the Fair!
- Noah (Kingdom Kidz Bible)
- King Solomon (Kingdom Kidz Bible)

- Zacchaeus (Kingdom Kidz Bible)
- Martha and Mary (Kingdom Kidz Bible)
- Moses (A Bible Touch Book)
- Jonah (A Bible Touch Book)

Beginning Readers and Chapter Books
- *Parables in Action Series:* ***
    o #1 Lost and Found
    o #2 Hidden Treasure
    o #3 Comet Campout
    o #4 Moon Rocks and Dinosaur Bones
    o #5 Cooks, Cakes, and Chocolate Milk Shakes
    o #6 The Super Duper Seed Surprise
- *Marshal Matt Series:*
    o #1 Marshal Matt and the Slippery Snacks Mystery
    o #2 Marshal Matt and the Case of the Secret Code
    o #3 Marshal Matt and the Topsy-Turvy Trail Mystery
    o #4 Marshal Matt and the Puzzling Prints Mystery
    o #5 Marshal Matt and the Case of the Freezing Fingers

Middle Grade Novels
Black Patriots in the American Revolution, 4-book series

Nonfiction for Kids

- America's Black Founders: Revolutionary Heroes and Leaders with 21 Activities
- A Kid's Guide to African American History
- Old Testament Days
- Black Abolitionists: Lighting the Way to Freedom

Educational Market

- Reader's Theatre for African American History*
- WriteShop® Primary: An Incremental Writing Program—Books A, B, and C
- 15 Cut & Paste Mini-Books: Math
- 15 Cut & Paste Mini-Books: Science
- 15 Cut & Paste Mini-Books: Around the Year
- 26 Read and Write Mini-Books that Teach the Alphabet
- 25 Read and Write Mini-Books that Teach Phonics
- 25 Read and Write Mini-Books that Teach Word Families
- Grammar Manipulatives Kids Love
- Munch and Learn Math Storymats
- Easy-to-Read Nursery Rhyme Plays
- 15 American History Mini-Books*
- 25 Science Plays for Emergent Readers**
- Math Mystery Mini-Books**
- 15 Easy-to-Read Neighborhood and Community Mini-Book Plays**

- 15 Easy-to-Read Holiday and Seasonal Mini-Book Plays**
- 15 Easy and Irresistible Math Mini-Books**
- 15 Easy-to-Read Mini-Book Plays**
- 15 Irresistible Mini-Plays for Teaching Math**
- Fresh and Fun: November
- Engage the Brain: Games: Grade Four*
- Brain-Compatible Math Activities: Grade Four*

Craft and Activity Books
- Unforgettable Edible Bible Crafts****
- Archy's Adventures: Colors, Numbers, Letters
- Red Hot Bible Puzzles
- Way Cool Bible Puzzles
- Cents-ible Bible Crafts
- My Book about Ben and Me
- My Book about Sara and Me
- Amazing Bible Puzzles: NT, OT
- Bible Crafts and More
- Jumbo Bible Bulletin Boards: More Bible Stories Preschool & Primary
- Jumbo Bible Bulletin Boards: Fall & Winter Preschool & Primary
- Favorite Bible Heroes for Ages 4 & 5
- Bible Crafts on a Shoestring Budget Grades 3 & 4

*Co-author Jeff L. Sanders
**Co-author Sheryl Ann Crawford
***Co-author Susan Titus Osborn
****Co-author Nan Williams

Index

Breinigsville, PA USA
23 October 2009
226404BV00001B/83/P